INTRODUCTION TO FINANCIAL SERVICES

The Giving of Financial Advice

Ted Lake, ACIS, ACIB, ASFA

OLD BAILEY PRESS

LAW IN PRACTICE SERIES

OLD BAILEY PRESS
200 Greyhound Road, London W14 9RY

© Ted Lake 1998

ISBN 1 85836 287 3

British Library Cataloguing-in-Publication Data

A catalogue record for this book is available from the
British Library.

5 4 3 2 1

Printed and bound in Great Britain

Contents

Contents

Preface

The financial services industry within the UK is already large and well established and seems set to grow significantly further over the next few years.

This book is aimed at those starting out in the industry at whatever age, as a complement to formal examination qualifications. The author cannot stress too strongly his belief in the practice of 'best advice' and the need to make every effort to satisfy fully clients' requirements.

Every effort has been made to ensure accuracy at publication, but the financial services industry is evolving constantly. Budget and other legislative changes are likely to affect some of the detail in this book and readers are asked to bear these in mind.

There is much information that the author wished had been available to him when he switched careers, from banking, in 1991.

The writer would welcome comments and suggestions that might be of use for a future edition.

Ted Lake, ACIS, ACIB, ASFA

June 1998

Acknowledgements

The author would like to acknowledge the help and advice received from the following people in the preparation of this book:

Graham Crossley, ALIA (Dip) and Martin Dickinson, ACIB, both practising IFAs, and John Dean, BA, MSc;

Carys Jones, Press Officer for National Savings;

IFAA, for permission to use their Factfind;

Micropal for permission to use some of their statistics;

Mr G M Enriques of H E Foster & Cranfield Ltd;

David Crystal, Area Manager of Skipton Building Society;

and particularly to:

Michael Drakeford, Head of Compliance at a major UK bank, who read the full text and made numerous helpful comments and suggestions;

and lastly to:

June Woolley, my secretary, for kindly typing the text and coping patiently with numerous amendments.

Definitions of Key Terms and Phrases

Deposit-based Investments:
(often referred to as 'Savings')

Bank and building society accounts; TESSAs; National Savings products. Capital values can never fluctuate and there is no 'investment risk'; the investment/deposit account is always represented by the sum lodged, plus, possibly, interest or other 'bonus'.

Asset-backed Investments:

Direct investments into stocks and shares and other stock-exchange-listed investments; units in unit trusts and units in life funds where the value is directly or indirectly linked to stock exchange prices; higher income bonds where the final return of capital is conditional upon the level of stock exchange indices; and money-purchase pension plans and FSAVCs.

FSA:

The important Financial Services Act 1986 is generally referred to as the 'FSA' in newspaper articles, reference papers etc.

When much of this book was already written, the overall regulatory authority announced its title as the Financial Services Authority. Although the same initials are used in both instances, the difference should be clear.

Best Advice:

Although these words have been used throughout and the general sense will be clear, there is now a trend for the use of less emotive terms, such as 'suitable advice' and 'good advice'.

Abbreviations Used in this Publication and within the Financial Services Industry Generally

ACII	Associate of the Chartered Insurance Institute
ADL	Activities of Daily Life
AFPC	Advanced Financial Planning Certificate
AGR	Annual Growth Rate
AIM	Alternative Investment Market
AITC	Association of Investment Trust Companies
ALIA	Associate of the Life Assurance Association
APMM	Association of Policy Market Makers
APT	Association of Policy Traders
ASU	Accident, Sickness and Unemployment Cover
AUTIF	Association of Unit Trusts and Investment Funds
AVC	Additional Voluntary Contribution
BA	Banking Act 1987
BES	Business Expansion Scheme
CBT	Computer-Based Training
CeFA	Certificate of Financial Advisers
CGT	Capital Gains Tax
CIB	Chartered Institute of Bankers/Capital Investment Bond
CIC	Critical Illness Cover
CIFA	Certificate of Independent Financial Advice
CII	Chartered Insurance Institute
CPA	Compulsory Purchase Annuity
CPD	Continuing Professional Development
CTP	Common Trading Platform
DAX	Deutscher Aktienindex (Frankfurt Stock Exchange)
DSS	Department of Social Security
DTI	Department of Trade and Industry
EIS	Enterprise Investment Scheme

EPP	Executive Pension Plan
EZPT	Enterprise Zone Property Trust
FIP	Family Income Protection
FLA	Finance and Learning Association
FPC	Financial Planning Certificate
FSA	Financial Services Act 1986/Financial Services Authority
FSAVC	Free Standing Additional Voluntary Contribution
FTSE	Financial Times 100-Share Index
FURB	Funded Unapproved Retirement Benefit
FWOL	Flexible Whole of Life
GIB	Guaranteed Income Bond
GIO	Guaranteed Insurability Option
GMP	Guaranteed Minimum Pension
HIP	Home Income Plans
IAC	Investment Advice Certificate
ICA	Institute of Chartered Accountants
ICS	Investors' Compensation Scheme
IFA	Independent Financial Adviser
IFAA	IFA Association
IFAP	IFA Portfolio
IFP	Institute of Financial Planning
IHT	Inheritance Tax
IMRO	Investment Management Regulatory Organisation
IPC	Investment Planning Certificate
ISA	Individual Savings Account
IT	Information Technology
KFD	Key Features Document
LIA	Life Insurance Association
LPI	Limited Price Indexation
LTC	Long-Term Care
MAR	Medical Attendance Report
MCA	Married Couples' Tax Allowance

MCRI   Mortgage Code Registry of Intermediaries
MER   Medical Examination Report
MIG   Mortgage Indemnity Guarantee
MIP   Maximum Investment Plan
MIRAS   Mortgage Interest Relief at Source
MPP   Mortgage Protection Policy
MPR   Mortgage Protection Repayment
MSI   Member of the Securities Institute
MVA   Market Value Adjuster
NRD   Normal Retirement Date
NRE   Net Relevant Earnings
NVQ   National Vocational Qualification
OEICS   Open-Ended Investment Company Shares
OMO   Open Market Option
PA   Personal (Income Tax) Allowance
PAYE   Pay As You Earn
PEP   Personal Equity Plan
PHI   Permanent Health Insurance
PI   Professional Indemnity
PIA   Personal Investment Authority
PIC   Personal Investment Certificate (?)
PLA   Purchase Life Annuity
PMI   Permanent Medical Insurance
PPP   Personal Pension Plan
PRI   Retail Price Index
PSBR   Public Sector Borrowing Requirement
PTD   Permanent Total Disability
RI   Registered Individual
RNI   Return of Contributions, No Interest
ROF   Return of Fund
RPB   Recognised Professional Body
RPI   Retail Price Index

RSP	Recurring Single Premium
RWI	Return of Contributions with Interest
RWL	Reason Why Letter
SERPS	State Earnings-Related Pension Scheme
S & P	Standard and Poor
SFA	Securities and Futures Authority
SHIP	Safe Home Income Plans
SIB	Securities and Investment Board
SIPP	Self-Invested Personal Pension Plan
SMF	Self-Managed Fund
SOFA	Society of Financial Advisers
SRA	Selected Retirement Age
SRO	Self-regulatory Organisations
SSAS	Small, Self-Administered Scheme
SUQ	Supplementary Underwriting Questionnaire
TESSA	Tax-Exempt Special Savings Account
VCT	Venture Capital Trust
WBPR	Waiver Benefit Past Renewal
WDD	Waiver Definition of Disability
WOL	Whole of Life
WOP	Waiver of Premium
WP	With Profits
WPE	With Profits Endowment
WPWOL	With Profits Whole of Life Endowment
ZDP	Zero-Dividend Preference Shares

Financial Qualifications

Financial Planning Certificate	FPC
Advanced Financial Planning Certificate	AFPC
Society of Financial Advisers	SOFA
Certificate of Independent Financial Advice	CIFA
Investment Planning Certificate	IPC
Associate (Member) of the Life Assurance Association	ALIA
Associate of the Chartered Insurance Institute	ACII
Member of the Securities Institute	MSI
Certificate for Financial Advisers	CeFA
Personal Investment Certificate	PIC

These qualifications (and certain derivatives thereof) enable their holders to obtain authorisation under the FSA, albeit at differing levels. Most, however, will be able to give advice on retail-packaged, branded products and basic pensions.

Generally speaking, authorisation to advise on direct stock exchange investments, portfolio management and more complex pension matters requires a higher qualification, usually issued by the MSI, an RPB or the Institute of Pension Managers; this also applies to advice on pension transfers.

1 The Purpose and Aim of this Book

The purpose of this book is to provide help and guidance on when and how to offer financial advice to members of the public. It is aimed principally at someone starting a career in financial services, or thinking of doing so. The book is not aimed at experienced advisers or those intending to advise the very wealthy or people keen to take high risks, although for completeness reference will be made to higher-risk investment opportunities such as EIS, VCTs, EZPTs etc.

The writer is an IFA with a firm of solicitors who believes that this book should assist both IFAs and those who choose to become 'tied', as well as those employed by life offices or product providers, and, possibly, financial journalists. From time to time reference will be made to the differences in the advice process for those who are tied and those who are independent.

The financial services industry in the UK is very well developed but is also subject to very tight control by the regulatory authorities. At the time of writing, the SIB in effect became the FSA; and the new, overall regulator has absorbed the authority of most other regulators (see Chapter 3). However, that is unlikely to alter significantly the advice contained in this book.

The implementation of the FSA 1986 created the need for IFAs, prior to which the concept simply did not exist. The years after 1986 witnessed dramatic growth in financial services, fuelled mainly by banks and building societies and some large direct sales offices. Various factors contributed. Public interest in personal finance was stimulated by the popular press, and in fact some Sunday tabloids abandoned stories of heroic pets and naughty vicars in favour of PPPs, PEPs and TESSAs! The privatisation programme of the 1980s further increased the public's interest and the number of private shareholder investors in the UK more than doubled. The pensions mis-selling saga contributed to a general awareness of the need for pension planning, and of the pitfalls.

The trend away from 'a job for life', and the growth of self-employment and 'contract' working means that financial advisers need to be fully aware of the range of protection products available and that they bring them to their clients' attention, even if that is not the initial financial advice sought. Thus an adviser needs to know about PHI, PMI and CIC, as well as the usual life, pension and investment products.

Pension planning must of course figure largely within any financial advice. Currently there is vague talk of the 'stakeholder pension', but SERPS is likely to be retained. So long as the tax benefits on contributions remain in place, pension planning must continue to be included when lump-sum investment advice is considered. All investment/financial advice should be given only after a proper evaluation of the tax implications, which usually means considering not only income tax but also the position relating to IHT and CGT. In some instances all three may be relevant to the advice offered.

The job is really about providing 'best advice' (which could be to do nothing!) and building lasting relationships with clients who seek regular advice.

For those advisers who get it right and take the time and the trouble to train and equip themselves to a high level and work to the highest standards, financial services can offer a very varied, interesting and rewarding career.

This book makes constant reference to a client's income tax position and the need for an adviser to have established this accurately. It does not set out to provide a comprehensive explanation of how the tax system works and how all liabilities are assessed, or how various reliefs can be obtained. That is well provided for elsewhere.

The book does not aim to give investment advice as such. Any reference to specific product providers or specific investment products is purely to give examples and elaborate on the matter being discussed. The writer is not attempting to tell anyone how to invest their money – that is already well catered for!

The material here will complement studies for relevant examinations such as FPC, AFPC and CIFA, and IAC.

2 Why Invest at All?

Many people are aware of the benefits of asset-backed investment. Others will say 'Why should I bother at all?', or 'Why should I take any risks?', or 'I have always saved with the TSB'! An adviser must therefore decide whether to explain the merits of asset-backed investment and whether it is appropriate for that client. For some it is clearly not and they would be better served by building society accounts. This is not to apply any criticism but merely to state a fact of life. Some people really cannot cope with risk and uncertainty; they are much happier with a passbook which shows to a penny exactly how much they have. To some, the concept of having only a scrap of paper evidencing units or shares with a variable value and uncertain income is wholly inappropriate, and, however evident the benefits may be to an adviser, pushing too hard may only result in upsetting the client. Such a client is probably better off with bank/building society/National Savings products, generally referred to below as 'deposit-based'.

Many people go through most of their working lives without really considering the benefits of investment as opposed to savings, only to be faced with the problem as a result of retirement or on receipt of a legacy or other windfall. The adviser must decide whether or not the client should consider asset-backed investment, and then take time to explain the subject fully, including the risks to capital and to income, the charges and the possible loss of liquidity.

It is the experience of the writer, and probably of most other advisers, that clients are shocked when shown the results of asset-backed investments and how well they have performed over the medium term. Indeed, average five- and ten-year growth figures are often greeted with disbelief, at which stage a cautionary approach is often needed to emphasise the short-term risks. Some clients need firm dissuasion from plunging too deeply into higher-risk investments. In addition, the current investment conditions need to be taken fully into account, and include:

- the future outlook for the economy generally;
- present and future inflation levels;
- political stability;
- currency risks;
- interest rates generally and likely future trends.

3

Most of the above is self-evident but needs to be borne fully in mind and linked to each particular client's time horizons and general attitude to risk and loss of liquidity.

On recommending that a client consider committing funds to asset-backed investments, it is worth setting out clearly the various aims and objectives of that decision, which could include:

- to aim to match or to beat inflation (see inflationary tables in the Appendices) – linked to aiming for capital growth, but not quite the same thing;
- to aim for a higher income than that currently available from deposit-based investments;
- to aim for an increasing income over the long term, say more than five years; this should often be a major consideration and there is a mass of data to justify that aim;
- to take advantage of all tax breaks available at the time;
- in times of high interest rates to guard against falling income should all funds be committed to deposit-based investments;
- in the medium to long term to aim for capital growth in excess of inflation.

Some investors will aim for several of these goals, but others will be more focused. It is critical that a financial adviser gets it right at this stage and establishes clear goals and priorities. All these aims and how they can be achieved are considered later.

3 General Background to Regulation of Financial Services in the UK

Until the mid-1980s sales of financial services products were largely unregulated. Many part-time workers were involved in selling insurance and investment policies, and many insurance companies were only too willing to grant agencies to them.

Inevitably this attracted those seeking fast cash via indemnity commissions and, without proper entry barriers, they soon found it possible to make large sums of money in a short time. Various scandals followed, in particular the failure of Norton Warburg, leading the Government to commission the Gower Report, which resulted in the Financial Services Act (FSA) 1986.

As is often the case, most honourable financial advisers with their clients' interests at heart were tarred with the same brush as were the unscrupulous minority.

The FSA 1986 is concerned with regulating the handling of investment business and sundry matters. It was enacted to promote honesty in the financial marketplace and to generate confidence in its operation and personnel. The Banking Act (BA) 1987 regulates the acceptance of deposits and affords depositor protection. The two regimes are not mutually exclusive in general, and many businesses require dual authorisation.

These are not the first Acts in these areas, but in many respects they go further than did their predecessors.

The purpose of the FSA 1986

This Act:

- regulates the carrying on of investment business;
- makes related provision with respect to insurance business and business carried on by friendly societies;
- makes new provision with respect to the official listing of securities, offers of unlisted securities, takeover offers and insider dealing;
- makes provision regarding the disclosure of information obtained under enactments relating to fair trading, banking companies and insurance; and

5

- makes provision for securing reciprocity with other countries in respect of the facilities for the provision of financial services.

Securities and Investment Board

One of SIB's first actions was to draw up a statement of ten principles to which it expects all firms and advisers to adhere. All SROs' and RPBs' rules have to reflect these principles.

Integrity
A firm should observe high standards of integrity and fair dealing.

Skill, care and diligence
A firm should act with due skill, care and diligence.

Market practice
A firm should observe high standards of market conduct. It should also, to the extent endorsed for the purpose of this principle, comply with any code or standard as in force from time to time and as it applies to the firm, either according to its terms or by rulings made under it.

Information about customers
A firm should seek from customers it advises or for whom it exercises discretion any information about their circumstances and investment objectives that might reasonably be expected to be relevant in enabling it to fulfil its responsibilities to them.

Information for customers
A firm should take reasonable steps to give to customers it advises, in a comprehensible and timely way, any information needed to enable them to make a balanced and informed decision. A firm should similarly be ready to provide a full and fair account of the fulfilment of its responsibilities to each customer.

Conflicts of interest
A firm should either avoid any conflict of interest arising or, where conflicts arise, ensure fair treatment to all of its customers by disclosure, internal rules of confidentiality, declining to act, or otherwise. A firm should not unfairly place its interests above those of its customers and, where a properly informed customer would reasonably expect that a firm would place the customer's interests above its own, the firm should live up to that expectation.

Customer assets

Where a firm has control of or is otherwise responsible for assets belonging to a customer which it is required to safeguard, it should arrange proper protection for them, by way of segregation and identification of those assets or otherwise, in accordance with the responsibility it has accepted.

Financial resources

A firm should ensure that it maintains adequate financial resources to meet its investment business commitments and to withstand the risks to which its business is subject.

Internal organisation

A firm should organise and control its internal affairs in a responsible manner, keeping proper records and, where it employs staff or is responsible for the conduct of investment business by others, should have adequate arrangements to ensure that they are suitable, adequately trained and properly supervised, and that well-defined compliance procedures are in place.

Relations with regulators

A firm should deal with its regulator in an open and co-operative manner and keep the regulator promptly informed of anything concerning the firm that might reasonably be expected to be disclosed to it.

Although the SIB has now become the FSA, it seems likely that these principles will remain intact. All the current compliance rules stem from them and from the Financial Services Act 1986.

Financial Services Authority

At present the regulatory regime is being reorganised and a new, principal regulatory authority formed: the Financial Services Authority (FSA). This body will incorporate the functions of:

Securities and Investment Board	(SIB)
Personal Investment Authority	(PIA)
Investment Managers Regulatory Organisation	(IMRO)
Some regulatory powers of the Bank of England	
Building Society Commission	
DTI Insurance Directorate	
Registry of Friendly Societies	
Securities and Futures Authority	(SFA)

It appears likely that the FSA will delegate some of its monitoring powers to the existing Recognised Professional Bodies (RPBs), which are:

The Law Society

The Law Society of Northern Ireland

The Law Society of Scotland

Association of Chartered Certified Accountants

Institute of Chartered Accountants in England and Wales

Institute of Chartered Accountants in Ireland

Institute of Chartered Accountants of Scotland

Institute of Actuaries

Insurance Brokers Registration Council

The FSA will not assume its full authority until 1999 but has already inherited the SIB's disciplinary powers – and shown that it is not afraid to use them. In a damning statement issued in 1997 it criticised Prudential Assurance in the strongest possible terms.

The exact objectives of the FSA have yet to be determined fully, but it is likely to set up a Consumer Panel. Such a panel would advise the FSA on the implications for consumers of any new policies it develops. A point in favour of having one regulator is that it provides a single access from which consumers may get information and help. The FSA already has an enquiry line dealing with finance-related complaints and other problems. At the time of writing it cannot deal directly with such problems, but it can direct callers to the current regulator or Ombudsman.

The FSA will also handle complaints about financial services or products currently dealt with by eight separate ombudsman and arbitration schemes. All these operations will merge to form a single Financial Services Ombudsman scheme. It is proposed that all firms authorised by the FSA will have to join the scheme.

4 Independent Financial Advice or 'Tied' Advisers and Who Can Give Financial Advice

A major feature of the FSA 1986 was the introduction of the new concept of *polarisation*. Professor Gower believed that it was in the public interest for all advisers in future either to be totally independent or to become totally tied to a single product provider, and that in all future dealings, and when giving advice, their position should be made clear to all customers/clients/buyers at an early stage. The aim is that the public should be totally clear as to whether they are receiving independent or tied advice, the distinction to be made clear at an initial interview, when advisers hand over (or post) a 'Buyer's Guide' (now a 'Client Information Letter'). A specimen of each is provided in the Appendices.

This concept took a long time, indeed some years, to be generally understood by the public. An immediate and mostly unwelcome effect of polarisation was that the majority of banks, building societies and insurance brokers looked at the question of independence and decided that they had no alternative but to become tied. A few banks and building societies managed to provide independent advice for some years, but by 1996 all the major banks and the vast majority of building societies had accepted, somewhat reluctantly, that the problem of giving independent financial advice was too onerous, and became tied.

That development could scarcely have been in the public interest but is what occurred. The problems of providing independent financial advice are that:

- a much greater range of knowledge of all products is required, which is unnecessary for those who are tied;
- providing and demonstrating 'best advice' is clearly more difficult because IFAs must 'trawl' the whole market to locate the best/most suitable products, which a tied adviser does not have to do;
- adequate training and supervision are required; compliance with the regulations is more complex;
- the cost of professional indemnity is greater.

All these problems are reduced greatly if a bank, building society or broker decides to become tied, although the desire not to have to share commission and thereby maximise profits will have been relevant too!

It will be obvious to all readers an independent adviser must have full access to the market in all those areas on which he or she advises, eg pensions, unit trusts, life assurance, or capital investment bonds. This is costly, difficult and time-consuming. A tied adviser need only be fully conversant with one particular provider's products.

Advantages of independence

- Independence of action will appeal to many advisers (but it must encompass impartiality).
- Consumers are becoming more aware of the value of truly independent advice. There is evidence to support this in the financial press and in articles in journals such as the Consumer Association's *Which?*.
- An adviser is free to decide how to share commission and/or charge fees.
- Advisers can switch between product providers to follow best performance.
- There is no restriction on the range of products that an adviser can recommend (subject to authorisation).
- Independent advisers can develop and use IT according to requirements.
- Although there is a shortage of in-house training, the IFA sector is well served by courses, seminars and presentations organised by product providers.

Disadvantages of independence

- Knowledge of a greater range of products is required.
- Providing and demonstrating best advice is much more onerous and complex.
- Ongoing training and compliance with regulations is more onerous.
- The cost of PI is much greater.
- There may be some difficulty in coping with IT developments, particularly for smaller IFAs.

Advantages of being tied

- The range of knowledge needed is reduced; indeed, having only one product range to sell and thereby gaining expertise can be a further advantage.

- There are less onerous regulatory requirements to demonstrate best advice.
- There is no requirement (indeed, it is not permitted) to comment upon or evaluate other similar products.
- Representing a life office or bank assurer with a strong brand name or high street presence may carry more weight than being independent and producing a business card showing, for example, 'XYZ & Co, Independent Financial Advisers'.
- There is only one administration and commission system and a streamlined compliance regime.
- Regular in-house training is available.
- IT support can be customised for tied agents and their products.
- It may be possible to acquire capital via the purchase of an equity interest in the company, or by increasing the value of one's 'book' or practice.

Disadvantages of being tied

- There is no independence of action.
- An adviser can offer consumers only a reduced product range (variable, depending on the company).
- The operating environment may be overly regimented or restrictive.
- Some products may be uncompetitive or costly or have poor track records, but the tied adviser is obliged to promote them.
- Bad publicity concerning other tied salespeople can reduce sales.

Conclusion

Readers will have to decide how they might fit into the financial services industry. For the undecided it should be noted that many newcomers start in the tied sector and after some years transfer to the independent sector. Few move the other way.

The large, national IFAs and the IFA departments of the larger accountancy practices seem to be moving towards a salary-based advice service. When recruiting consultants the emphasis is focused increasingly on technical ability, experience and academic qualifications. Indeed, some employers already require the AFPC as a benchmark/standard for their IFAs.

However, it is virtually impossible to become an IFA without some kind of track record within the industry, unless associated with a private business that can provide basic training. Most small IFA firms cannot afford to support trainees who do not contribute to the business in the short term. Larger firms are able to choose between applicants and may offer very attractive remuneration packages. Many IFAs in recent years have decided to join 'networks'. A note on networks generally is included in the Appendices.

5 Income Tax Considerations

It has always been important that an adviser should not consider providing specific advice for a client until that client's tax position has been established. It will be clear that investment products most suited to the non-taxpayer will differ from those appropriate to the savings-rate taxpayer, and will be different again for the higher-rate taxpayer. If new investment income is to be generated, say from investing the proceeds of a legacy, then the commensurate new marginal tax rate will need to be established.

While it is outside the scope of this book to consider calculating individual tax liabilities, the general principles must be understood clearly and included in the process of advice-giving. This will have been covered by various examinations and internal training.

Many non-taxpayers are opposed to having to pay tax on any new investment income, however suitable that investment may be. The adviser will need to explain in detail that it is *total net income* that is important, even if some income tax has to be paid. Indeed, having to pay tax at the current savings rate of (only) 20 per cent is not a real disincentive to generating additional income.

For clients faced with an income tax liability for the first time or for those whose total income will attract tax at the higher rate, additional financial planning is necessary. Indeed, an income tax rate at 40 per cent on investment income is an obvious disincentive. In periods of low interest rates, net income is likely to be minimal.

Various avenues exist to improve a client's tax position and reduce the total tax liability and the marginal tax rate. The main ones are:

- the use of tax-efficient investment schemes, mainly PEPs, TESSAs and ISAs;
- the use of some National Savings products such as National Savings Certificates;
- for married couples to invest solely in the name of the non-taxpayer or the lower-rate taxpayer;
- for higher-rate taxpayers to invest in capital investment bonds and withdraw the '5 per cent per annum' tax-free income (dealt with below);
- for higher-rate taxpayers to question if they really need any (or more) investment income and, if not, to make growth-orientated investments;

- the use of offshore bonds, although there are drawbacks;
- the use of investment trusts, zero-dividend preference shares (ZDPs) whereby income is converted into low-risk capital growth, albeit with a possible liability to CGT, which can usually be avoided by careful timing of sales and the use of annual exemptions;
- additional contributions to a pension plan, which can remove or reduce liability to higher-rate tax.

The writer has found many clients to be appreciative of the time and trouble taken to demonstrate and calculate the tax savings which can be achieved by the use of these quite legitimate tax-planning measures. If investments are sufficiently large, quite dramatic income tax savings may result. Advice in this area needs care and judgment, and advisers may feel the need for some help or support.

Readers should be aware of the 'age allowance trap'. When taxpayers reach 65 and 75 years, or in the case of married couples when the older partner reaches one of those ages, they are eligible for greater personal tax allowance, or married couples' allowance. However, these additional tax allowances are clawed back when total income reaches a certain level (currently £16,200 per annum). The additional allowances are decreased by £1 for every £2 of income above that threshold; this means that the benefits are lost at an income of around £18,650 per annum per person (in the current tax year, 1998/99).

For income within those bands, however, the marginal tax rate is 34 per cent. Clients are rarely aware of this as it is not apparent in assessments issued by the Inland Revenue or PAYE Notices of Coding etc. Notice is only given that the age allowance has been reduced, and the overall effect is far from clear.

So, there is considerable scope here for the good adviser, aware of the age allowance trap, to suggest measures to avoid it. The use of some of the measures listed above will achieve that objective. Realistically, however, clients of that age group and income level are unlikely to welcome schemes that depress income unduly, whatever the tax benefits. For most, the best options will be:

- the use of PEPs, TESSAs and ISAs;
- equalising a married couple's income to below £16,200 per annum;
- the use of single-premium insurance bonds and drawing the 5 per cent per annum tax-free income; all such income is treated by the Inland

Revenue as 'return on capital' and does not count towards the ceiling of £16,200 per annum.

Consideration of Capital Gains Tax (CGT)

It is outside the scope of this book to cover fully this complex matter. However, the possible CGT advantages of PEPs (and, probably, ISAs) will be of little benefit to most investors while the PEP allowance is £6,000 per annum and the annual CGT exemption limit is £6,800. Nevertheless, there are clients who in time will be likely to have a CGT liability. The potential CGT benefits for such clients should be borne in mind when formulating investment recommendations, and be noted fully in the file, letters and reports.

The CGT benefits of VCTs, EIS and EZPTs are dealt with later.

When advising on the possible sale of an investment, the potential liability to CGT must of course be borne in mind. The adviser may have to refer to a stockbroker or tax adviser for help. The important thing is to be aware of the dangers.

The acquisition price for all quoted shares and unit trusts held prior to 31 March 1982 was rebased upwards from that date. Since then, indexation has afforded a dramatic and beneficial effect for earlier years of high inflation. At the time of writing inflation is around 3 per cent per annum and seems likely to remain low, so for assets acquired in recent years the beneficial effect of indexation is much less. Losses can no longer be indexed upwards. Indexation of gains ceased as at 6 April 1998 and has been replaced by complex, tapering relief over ten years.

In 1996/97 the flotation/demutualisation of some building societies and life offices resulted in some clients holding shares worth £20,000 or more. If such shares were placed in PEPs at the time of issue, they may of course be sold free of liability to CGT. However, many holdings were not tax-sheltered in this way, so the possibility of a CGT liability should be considered. The Inland Revenue announced that it would regard the cost at acquisition as nil, so, except for PEPs, full sale proceeds will be 100 per cent gains and thus liable to CGT in full, less any indexation and less the current annual exemption.

Tables of month-by-month indexation allowances are published regularly in the press. The writer takes care to file these regularly so that effects of indexation may very easily be established.

Consideration of Inheritance Tax (IHT)

As with CGT, a detailed consideration of IHT is outside the scope of this book. However, good financial advisers will need knowledge of:

- the current IHT threshold (£223,000);
- the IHT rates of tax (40 per cent on estates above £223,000);
- how to advise clients likely to incur an IHT liability, and the point at which this and IHT-avoidance schemes should be considered fully.

Some basic topics inherent to the advice-giving process need to be borne in mind:

- Ensure that trusts are set up in respect of large PPPs.
- Ensure that proceeds from large life policies are directed to the beneficiaries via a trust, to avoid additional liability to IHT should lump sums be paid into the estate of the deceased.
- Consider the possibility of directing to children or grandchildren some of any new money to be invested for older clients.

Bear in mind that in these areas co-operation and liaison with clients' solicitors is desirable, and possibly the best way forward. As a separate but connected note, any major change in a client's circumstances, say receipt of a legacy, could mean that an existing will should be revised or updated, particularly if an IHT liability arises for the first time.

6 Investment Products including Retail Branded, Packaged Products

For the purposes of this book it is assumed that advisers are aware of the principal features of all the investment opportunities available, and therefore that it is not appropriate to set out an in-depth analysis of all or any of them. Such information will have been covered in training or other courses and when studying for examinations.

The writer is aware that the majority of advisers are limited in the range of products on which they can advise, and that such limitation is imposed by the very nature of being tied, or by the level of their own authorisation, or both. Most advisers, for instance, cannot recommend direct investment into the Stock Exchange via shares, or the use of gilts, and are restricted to pensions, FSAVCs and retail-packaged products.

Nevertheless, *all* advisers should have a basic knowledge of and be able to recognise those areas most appropriate for a particular client, even if such products fall outside their own area of expertise and/or authorisation.

The general range of savings and investment products available in the UK is broadly as follows. Products marked * may be 'regulated' if they contain any investment content, as opposed to being protection-only policies.

Savings schemes (not regulated by the FSA):
bank and building society accounts and deposits;

TESSAs;

National Savings products.

Retail branded, packaged products (regulated products):
unit trusts (whether in a PEP or not);

capital investment bonds, including distribution bonds and with-profit bonds;

unit trusts and investment trusts savings plans (including PEPs);

pension plans (including FSAVCs);

unit-linked savings plans (including MIPs);

Personal Equity Plans and Individual Savings Accounts;

endowment policies;

flexible whole-of-life policies;

annuities*;

back-to-backs;

friendly societies' products;

guaranteed income bonds and growth bonds;

higher-income bonds;

various tax-saving schemes, including EIS*, VCTs* and EZPTs*.

(See Chapter 22)

Products requiring a higher level of authorisation:
British Government gilts;

direct Stock Exchange investments;

single-company PEPs;

possibly those above marked *.

More complex pension arrangements:
executive pension plans;

SIPPs;

SSASs;

group pension schemes;

defined benefit salary schemes;

FURBs.

Products outside the scope of the FSA, ie unregulated:
mortgage protection policies;

level term policies;

convertible term policies;

family income benefit policies;

critical illness policies*;

permanent health insurance policies*;

private medical insurance;

long-term care policies*;

mortgages (although the repayment vehicle may itself be regulated).

No mention is made in this book of any of the following investments, which are outside its scope:

futures and options;

traded options;

currency funds;

land and property.

Investments of intrinsic value are not 'investments' within the meaning of the Financial Services Act, eg:

vintage cars;

wine;

precious metals;

paintings and other works of art;

stamps and coins.

7 Insurance Products for Protection

Most advisers will be fully aware of the broad range of protection policies available and will have received guidance and training through examinations and internal training courses on:

level term policies	convertible term policies
flexible whole-of-life policies	family income benefit policies
low-cost endowment policies	critical illness policies
PHI income protection policies	private medical insurance policies
accident and sickness policies	mortgage protection policies
mortgage payment protector policies	

There is general agreement that most people in this country are under-insured, particularly those with dependants. Clearly, effecting full cover for all life's risks is rarely affordable. Some factfinds are designed to highlight the need for various types of protection, but others are not. Many people are adamant that existing life cover built into their mortgage and linked to their pension plan is adequate. Advisers will need to probe thoroughly to establish the actual levels of cover in place, and if necessary offer to illustrate the shortfalls.

It will then be necessary to draw the attention of wage-earners to the risks that they run, particularly if they have young families. Those risks can often be broken down as:

- the effect on the survivors of the death of the main or only earner;
- the effect of the prolonged illness of the only or main earner;
- the effect of serious accident or permanent disability.

Advisers will be aware that this is a difficult area to deal with. Many people prefer to ignore the matter completely or adopt an 'it won't happen to me' attitude. However, those who are more realistic can usually be helped and advised on the protection of their families.

The cost of term cover has fallen dramatically in the last few years and the principal providers now offer high levels of cover for very reasonable premiums, provided the period is not long enough to increase greatly the insurer's risks.

Clients can often increase cover and maintain reasonable costs as follows.

- If an endowment policy is to be effected to repay a mortgage, usually CIC can be added at very little cost.

- A second life can often be added to an endowment policy at little extra cost.

- If term cover in a modest sum is required for a minimum premium, significantly greater cover can often be obtained for little extra cost.

- If cover is required for, say, a bank loan for the self-employed, who may also need additional life cover for other reasons, arranging convertible cover at the outset may be sound advice.

The main point to bear in mind is that an adviser should think carefully about who is to be protected and against what. The obvious solution may not be the best option, so time and trouble should be taken to examine all forms of protection policy applying to the client and/or the client's family. This may mean obtaining numerous quotations to try to obtain the best overall value for money. Those with access to the Exchange and the Common Trading Platform would be able to produce a wide range of quotations in, say, 15 minutes.

For the purposes of this book it is assumed that all readers are aware of the difference between guaranteed and reviewable contracts and other protection products.

The writer has not dwelt at any length on flexible whole-of-life contracts. For some people they offer massive initial cover on overall 'maximum' term but the investment element is very small, although better on a standard term. The author does not like mixing protection contracts with savings contracts, but the significance of the ten-year review period should be borne in mind and fully explained to the client, who should be left in no doubt that the very large initial cover will probably be much reduced at the first ten-year review.

Family income benefit policies offer cheap protection for families where a low premium is a necessity, but again a claim within the last couple of years in the life of the policy might result in only modest total benefits being paid.

Sales of CIC policies have been outstandingly successful in the last few years. Such policies have the attraction of relative simplicity. A CIC can be free-standing or added to other protection policies. However, care is needed to ensure that clients do not think that they have a PHI contract!

Sales of PHI (income protection) policies continue to be at a very low level. When the Government changed Invalidity Benefit to Incapacity Benefit in

April 1995, reducing the benefits and making them harder to obtain, the writer wrote to all relevant clients and drew their attention to the changes. The response was almost nil. People just don't think it will happen to them. The only way to sell PHI is by face-to-face meetings only with those willing to face reality.

Private medical insurance (PMI) is often easier to sell than PHI. People are all too aware of the problems facing the NHS at present, as waiting lists grow, and the benefits of PMI policies are therefore easier to quantify. There are now about 40 providers with around ten products each, so there is a bewildering range for an adviser to research. *Money Management* carries out regular reviews of the market, which are an invaluable aid. Generally, there are four types of product:

- top-of-the-range 'Rolls-Royce' plans – usually very expensive;
- standard plans;
- budget plans;
- special plans which pay out only if the NHS is unable to offer treatment within (usually) six weeks.

The writer usually recommends standard plans, certainly for those in work, and particularly for the self-employed. Some budget plans may be acceptable to retired people who need to minimise costs. Most special plans have been withdrawn recently as only emergencies are dealt with by the NHS within the timescale!

Not all advisers will wish to handle PMI plans and, indeed, some tied advisers may be prohibited from so doing. Commission earnings are very modest. Nevertheless, some clients may seek advice on these products and most professional advisers would wish to be able to offer help and guidance.

8 Investment Risk I

Anyone offering investment and financial advice must be prepared to tackle the question of risk at an early stage. This may seem obvious to some but less obvious to other readers; but more importantly, clients may not have thought through how any risk might apply to them. The writer can point to three distinct areas where risk needs to be considered separately:

1. Pension planning: the risk is obvious to advisers, namely that of not having provided for one's retirement years.

2. Personal risks: of death at an early age and the effect of serious accident or illness, reducing ability to work and to earn.

3. Investment risks: inherent in any asset-backed investment are risks to capital or to income, or to both.

Pension planning

This is generally the most straightforward area for an adviser to tackle. Some basic facts are worth remembering and using where appropriate:

- Most people would like the opportunity to retire early.
- Most would like the opportunity to retire at the time of their choosing.
- Few relish the prospect of a long retirement on inadequate income.
- Life expectancy has increased by 12 years during the lifetime of the writer and seems set to increase consistently in the future.
- Early retirement is now a fact of life with vast numbers of people retiring, either voluntarily or compulsorily, during their 50s.
- Taken together, the last two points will result in many people having up to 30 years in retirement.
- The earlier a person retires, the more active that person is likely to be, and hence a better income will be needed to sustain that lifestyle.
- The State pension is likely to continue to lose its value in real terms. Some years ago it was equivalent to 21 per cent of average earnings but has now dropped to 14 per cent; the generally held view is that it will fall to 9 per cent by 2020.
- The future of SERPS is uncertain.

All the above is mostly beyond dispute and points to the same, clear conclusion: that sensible and prudent people should take time to consider their existing pension arrangements. This may prove to be a painful exercise when current pension rights and likely projections are examined.

Many pension projections are to a NRA of 65, but when clients are asked how many people of that age are working in their organisation, the answer often is 'none'. When asked how many are still working at 60, the answer may be 'none' or 'very few indeed'. Readers will know the effect of early retirement on final salary schemes.

Obtaining a revised projection of a money purchase scheme to, say, age 55 or thereabouts will put the whole matter into perspective.

The need for sound pension advice is clear, both when requested in its own right and when advice on lump-sum investments is sought. In the latter instance the adviser will usually establish what immediate and future capital expenditure is planned and earmark a prudent cash reserve, after which use of the remaining lump sum to top up a personal pension should be a priority. This advice may extend to a spouse's pension plan and could be achieved by utilising past, unused reliefs under 'carry forward' provisions. Indeed, for a 40 per cent taxpayer the justification for this recommendation is beyond question.

Personal risk

Here the risk and the need to insure against it falls into two distinct areas. First, protection of dependants will be met by life cover, either term or whole-of-life, with loss of income covered similarly or by a family income benefit policy. The point for the adviser to focus on and to quantify is the likely loss of income due to death. In most instances really large capital sums are needed to make adequate provision, particularly in respect of younger men expecting their incomes to increase as their careers progress. Further, loss of company cars and pension rights need to be included.

Secondly, there are the risks of serious illness or accident that reduce a person's ability to work and to earn. Such risks are protected by PHI, CIC etc. In this country there is a marked reluctance to effect income protection, although CIC contracts have become easier to sell within the last few years. Again, many clients seriously overestimate the degree of financial support they will receive from their employers and from the State.

The changes to legislation in April 1995 resulted in Incapacity Benefit being much harder to obtain, and made it taxable. Other changes include the DSS's requirement to meet mortgage interest payments being deferred for nine months. That alone could prove calamitous for some, and is another worry at an already traumatic time. Some life offices have produced excellent sales aids which set out in stark terms the reduced level of State support. The writer has some of these aids in a generic file on PHI that prove very helpful when advice is sought in this area.

Investment risk

This is harder to quantify and explain than are the areas dealt with above. The question of risk arises when advice is sought on lump-sum investments, or converting regular savings plans into unit or investment trusts, whether via PEPs or not. Some clients already holding shares or unit trusts will probably be aware of the investment risk, which will make the process easier. Nevertheless, investment risk is heavily linked to timescales and the client's short- and long-term plans both need to be established at an early stage.

In general terms, the longer the likely period of investment, the less the risk. There is a mass of data available that demonstrates the growth in asset-backed investments over periods of ten years or more. The author maintains a generic file showing in various forms the growth in share prices, the FTSE 100, unit trusts and CIBs over differing time periods, covering growth in capital and income.

This evidence is the justification for committing funds to asset-backed investments – certainly when viewed alongside tables on the effect of inflation.

However, the short-term risks remain and should be stressed very clearly. The writer vividly remembers 1994, a dreadful year for investments generally. Over that year capital values generally fell by about 10 per cent, some by more. Any investments made early that year, subject to the usual bid/offer spread of 5 per cent, resulted in horrendous capital losses of around 20 per cent – on investments that were promoted on the basis of lower risk. Fortunately, most of those investments have now recovered fully and investors are showing capital profits, but many advisers had worried clients at the end of that year.

It is the writer's practice to stress the effect of any initial bid/offer spread and the investment risks to all new investors and to make the general point that such investments generally should be made on a minimum of a five-year view. While there have been recent very good years, notably 1993, 1995, 1996 and 1997, when dramatic gains occurred within a matter of months, in general the risks remain. In considering with-profit bonds an even longer-term view should be contemplated if possible from the outset.

Another, and fruitful, way to approach and deal with investment risk is to focus on the effects of inflation. Although well under control and at a low level at the time of writing, it may rise in the future. This is not a recent phenomenon. Students of history will know that it was a major problem in this country in the reign of Queen Elizabeth I!

Some people faced with making lump-sum investments for the first time find they cannot cope with risk or uncertainty. They are only really happy with building society passbooks that show definite balances. The concept of exchanging a cash deposit for scraps of paper is just too much, as is the fact that they cannot readily ascertain a value (which may well have decreased). There is no real alternative to deposit-based schemes in these instances. For other, less risk-averse investors, a sensible route may be to recommend that 50 per cent or less be committed to asset-backed investments, with 50 per cent or more retained in deposit-based investments. That way they have a chance to 'test the water' and familiarise themselves with the concepts. If the adviser then provides six-monthly or annual reports or valuations and the investments increase in value, eventually they may feel more comfortable committing more of their cash to asset-backed investments.

Care needs to be taken if a client's time horizons are short or uncertain. Prudent advisers will point out that most asset-backed investments should be made on at least a five-year view. In instances of arranging investments on trust for a minor, the time span will be known precisely and they can be planned accordingly.

An additional problem with time horizons is in advising the very elderly. Men of about 70 have sometimes remarked: 'I am too old for any real investments at my age.' The writer keeps a mortality table in his desk and is able to reply along the lines of 'You have a life expectancy of 15 years, so I think that you are a long-term investor!'

Clearly, this has to be handled very tactfully and restraint is needed when clients are in poor health. Hence the inclusion in this book of material on Factfinds. A lady aged 80 in good health has a life expectancy of 8.4 years and could therefore consider a with-profit bond. Linked to risk and aims and goals is the need and desirability of asking new clients if they are thinking solely about themselves or whether they wish to maximise their estates for the ultimate benefit of children and grandchildren. The majority are keen to do the latter, particularly if they have benefited from legacies.

As a result of such approaches some clients in their 70s or 80s may decide to commit funds to asset-backed investments instead of leaving them in building society accounts.

As mentioned above, overall risk can be reduced by retaining funds in building society or similar accounts. However, if asset-backed investment is to be effected, the overall risk can be managed by varying investments and committing different proportions to each. Clients could be asked: 'How much risk is acceptable to you on a rising scale of 1 to 10?' The scale/staircase of investment risk is set out in the Appendices. The writer has found this approach generally to be helpful – most new investment clients can relate to the chart. When faced with the question most indicate a risk range of 3–5.

Those who are totally risk-averse usually make it very plain at this stage, as do those who will accept an above-average level of risk.

It is vital to ensure full disclosure of risks and to take steps to ensure understanding by the client, and to provide all relevant data in an RWL or investment report.

In arranging larger portfolios, the writer often groups investments into the general areas of very low risk, low risk, medium risk, and higher risk. It may be appropriate to show percentages against each category. Most clients can understand and relate thereto and are capable of indicating whether or not the proportions are acceptable, and also whether the overall risk profile meets their needs.

9   Investment Risk II

There is a likelihood that new young recruits to the financial services industry may fail to understand and sympathise with a prospective new investment client's concerns about risk.

Some people have an inherent fear of investment risk, just as others have phobias about, say, flying, lifts or water. The remedy might be to demonstrate:

- track records of appropriate products against the risk to capital of inflation;
- how overall risk can be reduced by the use of lower-risk products and by retaining funds in deposit-based investments.

A useful aid could be graphs showing the rise in share prices and indexes generally over a period of years. The writer has a range of performance charts going back 10 to 20 years, and some to as far back as 1945 and 1900!

All the above help to demonstrate that, over time, asset-backed investments generally have kept pace with and comfortably beaten inflation. Investment risk gets less as time passes, as investments make up any initial bid/offer spread and appreciate in value if given sufficient time. The vast majority of collective investment schemes increase in value, although performance varies greatly. The main point to bear in mind is that concerned, first-time investors can be reassured that provided they take the medium-term view of five or more years and provided they have adequate deposit-based cash reserves, investment risk can be reduced to a tolerable level.

This point can be expanded upon by advising that if and when investments show a reasonable profit, some or all of that profit can be removed to a secure base, which will simultaneously reduce overall investment risk.

Younger advisers may be reluctant to acknowledge some prospective investors' fears, possibly because of the wish to secure the business, or the view that the client is over-cautious. There is no easy solution to this other than to note the general points that follow.

Advisers need to be very clear about the degree of risk to which the client's funds are to be exposed, and the relative degree of risk attaching to different investments. Some clients understand the risks and can give adequate guidance to an adviser. Others, or first-time investors, cannot. Risk is a bit like pain: when it is there you know about it, but it is always difficult to quantify.

Comment has been made earlier about discussions on risk when completing a Factfind, and the use of the 'staircase of investment risk'. The following should also be noted:

- UK equity income and equity growth unit trusts, investment trusts and life funds carry 100 per cent of the risk attached to the UK equity stock market.

- Managed funds carry less risk because of the inclusion of fixed-interest stocks and gilts.

- Cautiously-managed funds carry even less risk.

  Advisers should look carefully at the relevant pie charts to establish the investment spread, and form a view as to the overall risk run.

- Smaller company funds should offer greater potential for capital growth, but this has not been achieved in recent years. Income is likely to be low and performance will suffer further if the sector goes even more out of fashion. Such funds must therefore carry a higher risk than the ones mentioned earlier.

- Gilt, fixed interest and bond funds should be very low risk, *but* their make-up can vary widely. Generally, the higher the yield, the greater the risk to capital. High yields will be achieved by using lower graded bonds or preference shares, rather than gilts. The redemption date on gilts provides an additional safety factor not present with most preference shares.

  Any significant increase in interest rates will have an adverse effect on the market price of all bonds and gilts, as was seen dramatically in 1994.

- Distribution bonds vary considerably in their underlying portfolios, which has an effect on the risk factor. Some include commercial property, which should reduce overall risk. Again the investment strategy and make-up need to be investigated.

- With-profit bonds are generally considered to be very low risk because the price of the units cannot go down. There are two investment risks to bear in mind:

  i   The bonus rate, not being guaranteed, may be reduced.

  ii The *Market Value Adjuster* (MVA) can be used upon a full or partial withdrawal. A full explanation of the MVA is provided in the Appendices.

  The makeup of with-profit bonds varies. For instance, Scottish Mutual's with-profit bond has 73 per cent of its investment in UK equities, so overall performance should be good if stock market conditions remain favourable.

- International funds need to be subdivided into:
  i worldwide funds;
  ii wide geographical areas, eg Europe, USA;
  iii emerging markets;
  iv individual country funds.

A look at past performance of these international sectors may be helpful:

		Five-year AGR (%)	Ten-year AGR (%)
i	International equity growth	11.2	11.4
ii	USA only	14.7	16.2
	Europe only	17.4	15.6
iii and iv	Average of all emerging markets' unit trusts including individual country funds	0.3	10.7
	UK equity income funds	15.2	12.6
	UK equity growth funds	15.7	12.0
	UK smaller company funds	14.4	9.7

(Source: Standard & Poor's *Micropal,* May 1998)

While a broadly based international fund should be low- to medium-risk, a single-country fund in the Far East or in Latin America will be near the top of the staircase of investment risk because it will carry:

- very high inherent investment risk;
- currency risk;
- political risk;
- low income;
- high volatility.

It therefore seems that single-country funds in emerging markets are really only for those clients who can understand and accept the attendant high risk and volatility. Global emerging market funds should reduce significantly the investment and political risks.

The UK stock market has been very successful in recent years and looks set to rise further now that the growth in the USA economy has effectively wiped out the PSBR.

Europe has been a very favourable market for investors over the last few years, as the above figures demonstrate.

The risk attached to high-income bonds

In the period 1996/98 high-income bonds typically offered around 10 per cent per annum net of tax, paid monthly and fixed for five years. Return of capital depends upon one or more financial indexes not being lower at the end of that period. The indexes used, either solely or jointly, are usually the FTSE 100 Index, the S & P 500 Index and the DAX. As a lower-risk variant, some high-income bonds offer a lower rate of return but guarantee full return of capital provided that the indexes used have not declined by more than, say, 15 per cent.

Numerous sales aids have been prepared by companies promoting high-income bonds indicating that statistically the risk of the indexes falling is very remote. There have been other articles in trade journals, and more particularly in the financial press, pointing out that the promotion of such high-income bonds 'is a guaranteed scandal'.

There is no doubt that there is some risk attached to these bonds, although the risks are hard to quantify.

It has been the writer's experience that some more knowledgeable and experienced investors seem quite willing to take that risk, which they perceive to be very small indeed. The attraction of such bonds is that, at the time of writing, with building society monthly income accounts of £10,000 to £25,000 averaging taxable returns of 7.3 per cent, a high-income bond offering 10 per cent net represents almost a doubling of net income after tax.

It is the writer's personal view that:

- There is certainly some risk.
- The risk should be carefully explained to the client. If the client is nervous or cannot accept the risk and uncertainty, the matter should not proceed.
- If the investment is to proceed, the degree of risk should be spelt out most carefully in a 'reason why' letter (RWL), clients being given every opportunity to change their minds.

- If the investment is to proceed, the amount committed to that type of investment should be reasonable in relation to the client's investment portfolio.

Index tracker funds

These unit trusts set out to 'track' a particular index instead of being actively managed. They are promoted and marketed on the basis that numerous fund managers fail to match the performance of the FTSE Index and that managed funds carry relatively high management charges. Index tracker funds are not actively managed as such and therefore annual management charges tend to be less. At the time of writing there has been a maximum of only two years' past performance figures available for the majority of tracker funds, and during those two years there have been excellent stock market conditions which have, of course, been most favourable to tracker funds.

There seems to be quite a wide variation in performance of tracker funds, as the following table shows.

FTSE 100 tracking unit trust and OEICS (to 2 February 1998)		
	One year (%)	Two years (%)
FTSE 100	27.7	45.2
Direct Line	30.8	n/a
Scottish Widows	30.6	n/a
NatWest	30.3	n/a
Guardian	29.5	n/a
Fidelity	29.4	52.2
River & Mercantile	29.2	52.5
HSBC	29.0	50.5
Commercial Union	26.8	n/a
Midland	23.3	43.6
Equitable	23.2	n/a
Mercury	23.0	43.8
Barclays	22.1	41.6
Lloyds Bank	21.9	41.2

Sovereign	21.6	41.0
Govett	18.4	38.8
Foreign & Colonial	11.3	n/a
Average	*25.23*	*45.37*

(Source: Standard & Poor's *Micropal*)

FTSE All Share tracking unit trusts and OEICS (Offer to bid net income reinvestment to 2 February 1998)		
	One year (%)	Two years (%)
FTSE All Share	24.9	46.3
Legal & General	23.9	37.6
Virgin	23.8	44.7
HSBC	23.4	44.0
Dresdner	23.7	44.2
Gartmore	23.3	43.6
Old Mutual	21.1	32.8
Hill Samuel	18.9	38.8
Schroder	18.7	39.3
Norwich	17.6	37.8
Royal & Sun Alliance	17.6	36.1
Morgan Grenfell	16.4	34.5
Average	*20.7*	*39.3*

(Source: Standard & Poor's *Micropal*)

A point for advisers to bear in mind is that the attraction of these funds must, to a certain degree, be a matter of personal preference. There is a substantial amount of evidence that over the longer period, ie five years or more, the well-managed unit trusts and investment trusts significantly outperform the FTSE 100 Index.

It seems to the writer that many new investors have been attracted to tracker funds by a combination of good marketing, low charges and short-term good investment performance. There is a danger that many such investors may underestimate the inherent investment risk if the UK stock market suffers a setback. Therefore the real nature of tracker funds should be made very clear to new investors.

We shall just have to wait and see how trackers perform over the long term compared with actively managed funds.

10 Best Advice 1 – Factfinds

There is no generally accepted definition of best advice, nor are there any guidelines in the FSA. In many ways it is an unhelpful phrase because it implies that just one set of advice will constitute best advice and that variations will somehow fall short.

It is much easier to set out what is not best advice. For someone with little or no savings who inherits, say, £50,000, to tie up the total or make access difficult or expensive (however good the investments) is clearly not best advice. The wisdom of leaving a reasonable sum, possibly £10,000, in a building society account is unquestionable. Obviously less commission will have been earned, but that is what best advice is all about.

Best advice probably starts with the Factfind. The FSA does not include any specific requirement to complete a Factfind document, but one of the SIB's Statements of Principle is 'Information about customers': a firm should seek from customers it advises, or for whom it exercises a discretion, any information about their circumstances and investment objectives which might reasonably be expected to be relevant ...'

The need for a Factfind of some sort was always apparent to those giving investment advice, even before establishment of the FSA, but since then it has become a generally established, vital part of the advice-giving process.

Working through a Factfind at an initial interview and then retaining it has the advantages that:

- all relevant questions are asked and answers obtained;
- matters are not overlooked;
- the document then forms an integral part of demonstrating compliance as well as best advice;
- it is retained on file and will be useful in any future discussions;
- it is a sensible way of storing basic data which is unlikely to change very much;
- it is relatively easy to update from time to time.

There is no need for a Factfind to be signed, but many are. That is a matter of policy for each organisation. Some Factfinds are very long indeed, up to 20 pages. A specimen six-page Factfind is included in the Appendices by kind permission of the IFAA.

Completing a Factfind at an initial interview can take over an hour, but time spent in this area is usually worthwhile – indeed the majority of new clients are appreciative of the time taken and of so demonstrating a thorough approach. At a first meeting, completing the Factfind can open up possible areas for advice and action never originally anticipated. As a result of this exercise and a thorough approach, some or all of the following may need to be addressed:

- inadequate life cover;
- inadequate life cover on a repayment mortgage;
- inadequate pension planning;
- no PHI or CIC;
- inappropriate investments held which need reviewing;
- possible scope for tax planning/tax saving;
- a likely IHT liability.

In the case of older and wealthier clients, numerous other possible areas for advice often emerge. Although it may not be appropriate to tackle too much at once, it is often a good idea to include in a report the fact that various matters were identified as being in need of attention. That in itself goes some way towards demonstrating best advice and can provide a good reason to approach the client later, possibly when the main issue needing attention has been resolved.

Factfinds need to be updated from time to time to reflect all the changes in a client's circumstances. When such updates take place, the fact that it is an update should be noted clearly on the file, as that itself forms part of the compliance system.

As well as obtaining hard facts the Factfind exercise can cause clients to think carefully about their financial aims and goals.

Difficult clients

From time to time advisers will encounter the occasional difficult client who is less than open about earnings or about existing investments. It may be possible simply to annotate a Factfind with 'client declined to provide this information'. Being able to proceed without it will, of course, depend on the nature of the information concealed and the matter on which advice is being sought. Advisers will need to refer to their own internal rule book and to their compliance officer.

The writer recently received a general enquiry to advise about LTC and of course asked for a Factfind to be completed, albeit in broad terms. The client declined to provide any information but still wanted advice on LTC!

Without knowledge of income or assets the matter could not proceed further. If an adviser decides to proceed with less than full information from a difficult client, it is appropriate to include a reference to that lack of disclosure in a 'reason why' letter or other correspondence.

When dealing with a section in a Factfind on attitude to risk, the writer often finds the use of the 'staircase of investment risk' (specimen in the Appendices) a very useful way of helping clients deal with the concept.

11 Best Advice II

Having completed a Factfind carefully, an adviser needs to consider which areas to tackle and which products to recommend to meet the stated needs. When the need is clear and the client knows what he or she wants, the matter presents no difficulty. However, when there are several needs or a lump sum to be invested the matter becomes more complex. As a first step an adviser needs to be clear on the following areas:

- the balance of immediate needs against longer-term needs;
- attitude to risk;
- state of health and life expectancy;
- balancing conflicting aims;
- the client's ability to understand the nature of the investment product to be recommended.

Balancing immediate needs against long-term needs

This arises mainly in relation to lump-sum investments and the aim of balancing an immediate maximum income against a lesser initial income in the expectation of the benefit of an increasing income within, say, five years; an investor might expect this from a UK equity income unit trust. Some clients in their 60s faced with investing for the first time are apt to take a very short-term view. Here the adviser should demonstrate that good UK equity unit trusts have an impressive record of steadily increasing income over time and although the income from such investments can go down as well as up, historically it has rarely done so.

Attitude to risk

This was covered fully in Chapters 8 and 9.

State of health and life expectancy

Some clients will talk about this delicate area quite openly and honestly. Others are incredibly pessimistic and a few are certain that they are immortal. The point is that the adviser needs to think about this matter because it may have a bearing on investment decisions. Most Factfinds include a brief reference to state of health. In instances where state of health is obviously poor and impaired, to recommend longer-term investments may be questionable advice.

Some men around the age of 70 and in good health take the view that they are simply too old to consider Stock Exchange-linked, medium-term investments. The writer points out gently in these instances that if their health is good for their age they have a life expectancy of around 12 years and so by definition they are long-term investors!

Balancing conflicting aims

Balancing aims concerning immediate income is covered above. In the area of advice on protection, the problem usually arises when clients say that they have £100 per month available for pension provision and the adviser is asked to arrange that sum to best advantage. On investigation it may turn out that the client has little or no life cover and clearly some should be put in place to protect any dependants. The difficulty here is that every penny put into protection will reduce pension provision. That needs to be explained to a client and a decision reached on where the balance of advantage lies. To put every penny into a pension is to ignore the needs of dependants and could fall well short of best advice.

Clients' ability to understand investment products

Clients certainly do not need to become experts but a reasonable degree of understanding is desirable to avoid confusion over the aims of differing investment products, particularly the aim of investing for capital growth as opposed to income. There really is no solution to this problem except to say that in the experience of the writer it is a sound justification for the production of investment reports in the first place. Such reports typically explain a product in not more than two paragraphs and are much more likely to be read and understood than key-features documents (KFDs) or other product literature. In the case of typical unit trust investments, fact sheets are very helpful and, again, are usually easier to understand than KFDs.

Some clients are inarticulate and some others alter their aims or views from one meeting to the next. The writer recalls a wealthy lady client in receipt of very substantial income, well into the 40 per cent tax bracket, who agree to effect a PEP and was adamant that income was needed. A couple of months later, when effecting another PEP for the next tax year, she changed her mind and said that income was not required and could therefore be accumulated. Such instances make the task of advising more difficult; therefore clear file notes should be made.

Many clients seem to be overly concerned by the need for liquidity and or instant access to all or most of their investments, although in the experience of the writer very few want to make withdrawals of capital. However, it is desirable to make clear when providing investment advice which investments are:

- totally liquid/available although the unit/share price at the time is unattractive;
- available only after a set period of notice;
- available only subject to a penalty or an exit charge;
- available, but early withdrawals may mean the loss of guarantees as to capital protection at maturity;
- available, but withdrawals may lead to loss of tax benefits;
- not available.

Best advice is closely linked with professionalism

The essence of every true profession is that the practitioner puts the client's best interests first and does not recommend any course of action to better himself or herself at the client's expense. Put another way, however naive or willing a client may be simply to follow the advice offered, the adviser should not exploit this.

Examples of other than best advice include:

- Failure to provide for a reasonable cash reserve in a building society account. Commission will have been increased.
- All funds available being invested/tied up and failing to provide for a known capital expenditure. Again, commission will have been maximised.
- A non-taxpayer being advised to invest funds in a guaranteed income bond where the income is paid net of tax. The tax deducted can never be reclaimed.
- A non-taxpayer being advised to invest funds in capital investment bonds; tax is paid within the fund, but they are, of course, very high commission earners. Investing funds in a similar unit trust instead might be more suitable for the client and contain tax advantages, but the commission earned will be significantly lower.

- Inappropriate advice on repaying mortgages and effecting an endowment policy, when the period of time is obviously too short or the client's lifestyle clearly less than stable.
- In the area of pension advice it is easy to overstate the likely benefit that may accrue at NRD.

Full disclosure should reduce the incidence of clients overestimating the size of future pension benefits, but the dangers still remain because of unscrupulous advisers and/or naive clients – certainly when long-term projections to an unrealistic NRA are made. It is really misleading to produce a projection to age 65 when a client has no realistic chance of working above the age of 55. A 30-year-old male paying £200 per month would, at the standard growth rate of 9 per cent, generate a fund value of around £450,000 at age 65. That could be sufficient to provide a reasonable pension, but at age 55 the retirement fund would be only around £180,000 ie less than half.

All regular pension plans pay out relatively high commissions. Readers will be aware of the deceitful ploy of claiming a contribution meant as a single payment (commission about 5 per cent) as the first of a series of regular premiums. It may be that the practice has been eradicated, but the writer is not placing any bets.

Many clients cannot commit themselves to the regular monthly or annual contributions, or are getting close to NRA; in which case the best advice would be for them to pay recurring single premiums (RSPs). Total commission earned would be much less but the client's funds would be less depleted.

At the time of writing, the author is battling with a tied adviser who, incredibly, arranged a substantial additional mortgage for a couple, both aged 52, using a low-cost endowment policy over 18 years, when the man's clearly stated aim was to retire at 60. The high monthly premium would need to be paid to the age of 68 for all the benefits of the policy to be realised. As if that was not enough, the 'Advise' bolted on CIC and PHI benefits. A year later the clients realise how badly they were advised. The company's own compliance officer insists they have acted quite properly but the 'adviser' has moved on, having received an initial commission of around £2,500. A text book example of thoroughly bad advice.

In 1994 (a poor year for investments generally) some client farmers were persuaded by their high street banks to move £125,000 out of a high interest account and into the banks' own capital investment bond. They were pressurised and 'taken out to lunch'. Commission earned for completing just two forms would have been around £6,500. The bond suffered the usual bid/offer spread and lost value in the adverse stock market trends of that year. The clients then encashed the bond. The writer was asked to look into the matter and discovered that:

- the clients had no understanding of the bid/offer spread;
- they had no idea that the value of the units could go down and that they could lose money;
- they had no idea that the bond had no nominal rate of interest that they could compare with the bank or building society rate;
- they had no idea, and indeed were shocked to learn, of the size of the commission earned on the transaction;
- the bank put this large sum into just one CIB although the Factfind indicated a likely timescale of two to three years!

Measured by most professional standards, this was at the very least taking undue advantage by exploiting the bank's reputation and the clients' naivety and trust. It provides another good example of thoroughly bad advice.

The outcome was that the bank was quite unable to accept or to admit to giving poor advice in spite of an offer to settle the dispute on payment of a sum equivalent to the commission paid. The writer passed the case to the Investment Ombudsman who upheld the complaint; compensation of £22,500 was awarded.

To summarise, best advice is the combination of:

- thoroughly completing a Factfind;
- fully identifying a client's needs;
- producing the best solutions for the client;
- explaining solutions to the client, verbally and in writing, and establishing that proposals really do meet the client's needs;
- always making contemporaneous notes of any discussions with a client;
- putting the client's interests before one's own commission targets;
- implementing agreed investments.

12 Identifying Clients' Needs

Many existing or potential clients seeking financial help know exactly what they want, be it mortgage or pension advice or lump-sum investment. Some Factfinds have sections indicating needs, sometimes providing for more than one and sometimes indicating the client's own priorities.

In many cases the need is obvious. If somebody wants a mortgage, they don't necessarily at the same time want to start to consider their pension needs. Although they may accept that their pension arrangements are inadequate, it is unlikely to be the appropriate time to suggest taking on the additional commitment of an increased pension contribution. If the adviser identifies the need and/or if the client accepts the need, it is probably best to make a note in the diary and to take up the matter in, say, six or 12 months' time.

Similarly, those seeking pension advice are unlikely to be interested in lump-sum investments, and advisers need to explore the adequacy of life cover, family protection etc. Those seeking advice on regular savings may welcome a discussion on pension planning and the adequacy of life cover. It is helpful for an adviser to establish the reason for regular saving, ie to meet known or unexpected costs (holidays and/or school fees), to boost retirement planning or simply to save for its own sake. The response to enquiries will indicate whether further opportunities exist.

For those seeking advice on lump-sum investment the adviser needs to think widely. Although the initial meeting may, in the client's eyes, be solely to invest, say, £50,000 to best advantage, the adviser should take time to investigate:

- the need for adequate life cover;
- the need for adequate income protection;
- pension planning arrangements.

Only when those areas have been explored should attention be given to advising on investment of the lump sum. If either the first two is inadequate it might be that additional income could be generated out of the lump-sum investment to improve the cover. The author is dealing with such a case at the time of writing. The sum available for investment is around £80,000 and the client's wife, a mature student, expects to restart earning after 18 months. There are three teenage children, funds are now available to improve inadequate life cover for both partners, and the provision of income protection for the newly qualified wife seems desirable.

A reasonable level of additional income is needed for the next two years; thereafter the family income should improve, when the emphasis needs to be moved towards capital growth. The recommendations were:

£15,000	Scottish Mutual with-profits bond
£15,000	Sun Life deferred distribution bond
£12,000	Perpetual income fund in two PEPs
£5,000	Henderson European Value unit trust
£3,000	Stewart Ivory emerging markets
£50,000	
£10,000	Cash reserve
£10,000	Reduce mortgage
£10,000	Premium Savings Bonds
£80,000	

A client who leaves a secure salaried job to become self-employed or to start a business needs a range of financial products to replace some or all of:

1. Occupational pension plan;
2. Death-in-service life cover;
3. Occupational sick pay;
4. Private medical insurance.

All the above should be considered if possible, but to cover them all at an adequate level might prove too costly unless the client earns a very high income or is 'insurance minded'. The reality is that prioritising and compromise will be required according to the circumstances, available income and the client's attitude to risk. These separate areas should be considered as follows:

1. Restoring pension provision is an obvious need. Clients often like to put it off, but the writer feels that at the very least a start should be made in funding therefore, with a diary note made to review in, say, six or 12 months, depending upon the success of the career move.
2. Term cover to replace death-in-service cover is the first priority. At the present time this is relatively cheap, and if no cover exists a suitably large capital sum of between four and ten times annual earnings is required. Family income benefit plans can offer a cheaper solution.
3. Income protection for the self-employed and those earning a large

income 'on contract' is self-evident. All types of minor ailment and/or injury which might not prohibit those in full-time employment from working part-time could result in total loss of earnings on contract. The adviser will need to take into account the exact nature of the client's work. Clearly, a self-employed computer analyst might be able to work with a broken wrist but a dentist certainly could not! Similarly, the inherent risks in the workplace have to be borne in mind. Some jobs are wholly dependent upon the ability to drive a car. The writer has a self-employed chiropodist client who visits most of her clients in their homes. Inability to drive would stop her income instantly. On the other hand, a client running a substantial insulation and asbestos removal business with a good management team could, if necessary, oversee part of his business from home, with minimum attendance at work, for quite a long time. The business would undoubtedly suffer but a minor illness or accident would not be disastrous.

4. Private medical insurance was mentioned in Chapter 8. The need is linked to income protection and peace of mind in minimising absence from work (or from working normally) because of delays in obtaining medical treatment.

Identifying and meeting needs for lump-sum investments is usually fairly straightforward once the adviser has established:

- the cash reserve (if any) to be allocated;
- the cash (if any) to be added to pension plans;
- the length of time over which the funds can be invested;
- whether the need is to maximise income or to accept lower income, aiming for some capital or income growth, or both;
- the present and future tax position and the possible use of a spouse's tax allowances;
- the availability of tax saving schemes such as PEPs, ISAs, TESSAs etc.

The adviser can then construct a recommendation using the normal range of investment products.

13 Insurance Underwriting Affecting Clients

Underwriting can defined as *making sure that the premiums paid are relative to the benefits offered, ie the risks run.*

At a very early stage in providing financial advice, a new adviser needs to be aware of whether or not a product has to be underwritten, and requires a basic knowledge of the issues involved. Indeed, that is necessary in order to save possible later embarrassment when underwriting problems arise that could have been anticipated but were not, and result in the client finding that the proposed policy either is not available or is available only on more expensive terms. It is sometimes helpful to anticipate the problem and to tell the client that as a result of underwriting practice a premium may be loaded or the cover declined. That may avoid difficulties and resentment and result in a client accepting more readily a loading and a higher premium.

Some causes of underwriting problems are:

- medical conditions;
- hazardous/risky jobs;
- risky/hazardous pastimes/hobbies;
- extensive overseas travel;
- certain lifestyles.

An adviser needs to be aware of:

1. when full underwriting is needed;
2. when a lesser degree of underwriting may be acceptable;
3. where there is a maximum age limitation attached to a product; and
4. when a moratorium period on claims may be applied, although no underwriting is needed.

These areas can be identified as follows:

1. Full underwriting is applied on all conventional contracts of life assurance where death or serious illness or accident would trigger a claim and cause loss to the insurer, and encompasses:
   - all forms of temporary life assurance;
   - all whole-of-life contracts;

- endowment assurances;
- CICs and most PHI contracts.

2. A lesser degree of underwriting may be applied to:
   - some low-cost endowment proposals where amounts are not large and the applicants are below a certain age. Such proposal forms often ask only for answers to basic health questions, but adverse answers could lead to a more detailed range of questions;
   - LTC contracts that often call only for answers to limited health questions;
   - some ASU contracts that offer only very limited benefits and ask only basic health-related questions.

3. Maximum age limits apply at entry for most term assurances. Other investment products constructed around life policies impose a maximum age at entry are:
   - guaranteed income bonds;
   - MIPs;
   - CIBs and with-profit bonds.

   Maximum age varies from product to product and from company to company but is usually in the range of 75 to 90 years. This information is contained in product sales leaflets and in regular reviews of investment products which appear in *Money Management*. Additional information is available on all products in *Savings Market*.

4. Moratoria periods should not be confused with deferred periods, which are a key component of most PHI contracts. Some PHI contracts will accept all applicants, but a moratorium period will apply.

No underwriting necessity

In the majority of pure investment contracts where there is no life insurance, such as unit trusts, PEPs, TESSAs and PPPs (without life cover), the question of underwriting does not arise.

Single-premium life policies, eg CIBs and GIBs, have no underwriting requirements because the sums assured and repayable on death are usually between 98 per cent and 105 per cent of the initial single premium, so the investment 'risk' is minimal or non-existent. In the case of CIBs, once the units have appreciated in value and cover any initial bid/offer spread, that small risk is then totally removed.

Underwriting annuities

Annuities are not underwritten; indeed the reverse applies because the insurance company's risk is not the death but the survival of the annuitant for many years in excess of normal life expectancy at the time the annuity was purchased. No one in poor health would effect an annuity except for those with no choice, eg on retirement. But today an alternative to consider is drawing down income.

In times of high interest rates purchased life annuities might be an attractive option when all relative factors are favourable, but no one in very poor health would consider it to be a sensible investment; therefore the need for underwriting does not arise.

Annuities and impaired lives

Advisers should be aware that some annuity providers recently have been prepared to offer better-than-standard terms to provide annuities to those with major health problems, generally referred to as 'impaired lives'. Advisers should look out for regular reports on this topic in *Money Management*.

Waiver of premiums

The addition of a waiver of premium (WOP) to any contract will incur the need for underwriting. This requirement is most significant when a WOP is added to a PPP where no life cover is included. Obviously the pension provider has assumed a risk that was never there in the first place. In a PPP calling for large regular contributions by a younger person the insurance risk becomes significant. The adviser will need to consider the full circumstances of the client, as a WOP could be declined. However, if a WOP is declined, then at least the PPP can proceed without it.

Medical conditions affecting underwriting – family medical history

Most insurance proposal forms ask if any of the applicant's immediate family – mother, father, sisters, brothers – have died and, if so, the cause of and age at death. They usually go on to ask if anyone in the immediate family has suffered from heart attacks, strokes, cancer etc. The significance is that some of these medical conditions can be hereditary. This factor is particularly important when critical illness cover is applied for.

As a general rule, if one parent/brother/sister has suffered a critical illness before the age of 60 and no others have medical problems, the proposal can be accepted without a loading. If two members have suffered a critical illness before the age of 60, the proposal is usually accepted on receipt of a satisfactory medical report, and a loading may then be applied.

Existing medical conditions affecting underwriting

The following are examples of the more severe conditions that may be unacceptable, or that may require more heavily rated terms to be applied:

AIDS

Angina Pectoris

Aortic Valve Disease

Atrial Fibrillation

Cancer

Cirrhosis of the Liver

Cystic Fibrosis

Glomerulonephritis

Heart Attack (Coronary Thrombosis, Myocardial Infarction)

Heart Attack (requiring surgery)

Heart Failure

Hepatitis (chronic/active)

Hodgkin's Disease

Hydrocephalus

Intermittent Claudication

Kidney Transplant or Dialysis

Leukaemia

Major Organ Transplant (Liver, Pancreas, Heart and Lungs etc)

Mitral Valve Disease

Motor Neurone Disease

Multiple Sclerosis

Nephrotic Syndrome

Paralysis

Polycystic Kidney Disease

Stroke (Cerebral Embolism, Haemorrhage, Thrombosis)

Smokers

Smokers are charged higher premiums because of the statistical proof that smoking damages health and increases the risk of premature death.

Clients aged over 50

Clients over 50 years of age are more likely to have had or be currently suffering with medical problems and care should be taken when offering critical illness cover.

Lifestyle questionnaires and underwriting

The onset of AIDS in the 1980s caused great concern in the insurance industry, and rates increased dramatically in the belief that an epidemic was likely. In the event it did not occur and rates have reduced dramatically since around 1990. However, a practice has developed whereby acceptance of some proposals depends on completion of lifestyle questionnaires. An example is included in the Appendices. Although the practice of insurers varies, the general trend now is for completion of these when amounts are large. One leading life office applies these thresholds:

Single man	£100,000
Married man	£200,000

Some life offices' underwriters pay particular attention to divorced and single men, the latter above a certain age; those who spend time working abroad; and those who undertake unusually extensive foreign travel.

If the client fits into any of the above lifestyle categories, the insurance company will usually request a blood test and/or a doctor's report before accepting, declining or loading the premiums. Loading may be for a limited period of, say, five years. The writer recently managed to obtain life cover for a former drug addict (not intravenous) after doctors' reports and blood tests; the outcome was the wife being accepted at normal rates but a 50 per cent loading on the husband's premiums for five years.

Advisers should note that most life offices are somewhat coy about disclosing their precise attitudes and criteria in this delicate area and prefer to view each proposal on its own merits.

Underwriting limits

The larger the sum assured, the greater the medical evidence required, and as age increases so greater care is needed to reduce thresholds accordingly. The writer finds it helpful to keep a generic file on this aspect. From time to time data on all companies are published in trade journals. Individual companies occasionally amend their own limits, and as a result it is possible to build up profiles. Life offices' underwriting limits are in bands, by age and amount, and the typical range is as follows.

	XYZ Life Non-medical underwriting limits		
Age Next Birthday	Full Proposal Only	Medical Attendance Report	Attendance Report & Medical Examination
	£	£	£
Up to 40	Up to 90,000	90,001 to 180,000	180,001 and over
41 to 45	Up to 60,000	60,001 to 125,000	125,001 and over
46 to 50	Up to 50,000	50,001 to 100,000	100,001 and over
51 to 55	Up to 30,000	30,001 to 50,000	50,001 and over
56 to 60	Up to 15,000	15,001 to 30,000	30,001 and over
61 to 65	Up to 7,500	7,501 to 20,000	20,001 and over
Over 65	(refer to adviser)	(refer to adviser)	(refer to adviser)

Obtaining medical information

When necessary due to adverse medical information, age or large amounts, underwriters call for:

Medical Attendance Report (MAR)

completed by the client's doctor; no medical examination is necessary; and

Medical Examination Report (MER)

arranged and conducted by an independent doctor.

In all cases the medical fees are paid by the insurance company, even when the client is not required to attend.

Supplementary underwriting questionnaires (SUQs)

Most life offices have a range of SUQs; they form a first step to acquiring additional information before an MAR or an MER is necessary, although either or both could be called for subsequently. If an adverse medical condition is revealed on the proposal form it is sometimes sensible to obtain and complete a supplementary questionnaire and send it with the proposal. It can also often be appropriate to warn the client that the particular condition may cause underwriting difficulties. Tied advisers will have little difficulty learning when supplementary questionnaires are needed, and copies will be readily available. IFAs may decide to make a general file note on the range of supplementary questionnaires available from life offices they generally use. Although the practice of insurers varies, the following is a list of the usual supplementary questionnaires:

Asthma/Bronchitis or other Respiratory Disorders

Epilepsy

Gastric and Intestinal Disorders

Anxiety/Depression

Gynaecological Disorders

Back Disorders

Cysts, Growths, Lumps and Tumours

Thyroid Disorders

Diabetes

Activity questionnaires

These are called for when a pastime or hobby is classed as unduly dangerous, eg:

Parachuting

Mountaineering

Diving

Armed Forces

Motor Sports

Aviation

Some life offices have supplementary questionnaires covering some or all of these activities, to assist them in forming a view of risk.

Occupational hazards

A dangerous occupation may mean that permanent and total disability cover is not available. Common sense will alert the adviser. As a general guide, it may be helpful to look at the way occupations are viewed for PHI cover; if in Group 4, or if no cover is available, the occupation may be treated as hazardous.

Conclusion

Insurance underwriting is a skilled and complex business. It has been the aim of this chapter to highlight the main areas of likely difficulties for new advisers and assist them to at least anticipate and, perhaps, overcome those problems. It is not possible within this book to provide a comprehensive review of all aspects of underwriting.

Readers should also be aware that underwriting practices change with time. Some life offices offering the keenest rates for some types of cover may also adopt the tightest underwriting procedures.

14 Compliance

Overview

Compliance should not be confused with best advice. It is quite possible to provide best advice but for compliance to be totally lacking or inadequate. It is also possible (but less likely) to provide poor advice but for compliance to be perfectly satisfactory!

Who must be authorised

Section 3 of the FSA provides that 'no person shall carry on, or purport to carry on, investment business in the United Kingdom unless he is an authorised person ... or an exempted person ...'

This provision applies equally to banks, building societies, limited companies, partnerships, networks and to private individuals.

Compliance means that all authorised advisers must provide financial advice to their clients in accordance with:

1. the SIB's ten Statements of Principle;
2. their own organisation's compliance system, which should reflect the rules of the authorising SRO; and
3. their own level of authorisation.

In practice, this means that at the lowest level of authorisation across the industry most advisers, whether IFAs or tied, can give financial advice and arrange deals for investors/clients. However, tied agents may be restricted according to their knowledge and experience.

Generally, they may not: deal as principals with investors; deal with them as agents; or handle client money or assets.

Firms operating in the financial services sector are expected to have a 'compliance culture', which means that everyone within the organisation must be working towards fulfilling the requirements of the Financial Services Act.

What is compliance?

Compliance is effected by documentation and enforcement procedures facilitating companies to comply with the applicable rules and to achieve best practice. The regulators are looking increasingly beyond the strict wording of their rulebooks to see if firms are conducting their business in accordance with procedures and standards generally applicable in the marketplace. Hence, rules and guidance constantly change and will continue to do so.

Why is compliance important?

Compliance is an essential requirement in the sector. Increasingly, customers are asking to see copies of the latest regulatory reports on firms. Regulatory censure may lead to a fall in business confidence. Being a compliant organisation is good business practice. It implies that a firm provides the right service to the right clients, thereby minimising complaints. Last but not least, the FSA requires it.

Those who work for bank assurers, large direct sales organisations, large IFA firms and brokers, and IFAs in large networks will find that very precise compliance systems are now in place, so if they follow procedures compliance should not be too great a problem.

Those working for smaller IFA firms are more likely to encounter difficulties. Whatever the general standards of compliance, it seems to the writer that *all* advisers have a very clear duty to themselves, their clients and their own organisations to ensure that their compliance is satisfactory. If there is any doubt, additional file notes should be made or other data included to substantiate recommending a particular course of action and the justification for it.

The advisory process

At first client meeting

- Hand out business card
- Hand out client information sheet and/or terms-of-business letter
- Explain status, ie independent or tied
- Explain remuneration, commission system and fees
- Complete Factfind
- Establish client's needs and attitude to risk
- Seek agreement to proceed

Research

- Complete a meeting report form if appropriate
- Decide on products and recommendations
- Prepare report and 'reason why' letter
- Obtain quotations, factsheets and KFDs
- Prepare commission disclosure papers

At second client meeting or by post

- Explain financial recommendations
- Seek agreement to proceed
- If client does not accept advice, discuss and make any amendments
- If/when client accepts, send applications to product providers

At third client meeting

- Pass over contract notes
- Pass over certificates, policies and bonds
- Explain these items and possibly show clients where to locate unit prices in the financial press
- Discuss any future action
- Discuss a possible review date

In conclusion

- Check on compliance
- File records
- Make a diary note for any internal review
- Log client's investments on client's portfolio records if appropriate
- Check receipt of commission etc

Client files

Every client's file must contain:
- Factfind, plus additional relevant information in support
- Signed agreement or terms-of-business letter, or evidence that it has been sent

- Meeting report if appropriate
- Suitability notes
- Copy of financial report
- Copy of supporting data such as key features documents, providers' fact sheets, evidence of comparisons made, eg data from *Money Management* tables
- All correspondence
- Copies of all signed proposals/application forms
- Money-laundering compliance document
- Financial data to show movement of funds (for those authorised to handle client monies and documents)
- Evidence of receipt and disposal of documents of title
- Schedule of investments made
- Schedule of documents held (if appropriate)

Execution-only business

This is fraught with dangers if an investment turns sour and the investor is faced with a loss. In some cases investors have been known to approach advisers and say: 'I know that it may have been execution-only, but I fully expected you to warn me of the risks!' As a result some firms and networks will not handle execution-only business, except possibly with the prior approval of the compliance department.

The writer has experienced a few cases where potential investors wish to apply for public offers and have approached the writer's firm proposing that it affixed its stamp to application forms, thereby earning commission which could then be split with the investor. How such requests are handled is personal to the adviser relative to the company's own internal rules. Provided full file notes are kept and the matter is confirmed in writing to the client at the time, then at least the dangers are minimised, but readers should be very aware of the pitfalls.

If business is effected on an execution-only basis, the client should be sent a letter confirming this and the fact that no investment advice was provided, and further that the adviser accepts no responsibility.

Compliance on unregulated products

Readers will be aware that a wide range of financial products fall outside the scope of the FSA, particularly mortgages, PMI, PHI, LTC cover and term assurance. Some PHI and LTC products may be 'regulated' if they contain an investment element.

Many in the industry were surprised that mortgages escaped FSA regulation when the present compliance regime began. There is no real explanation for this other than that Professor Gower omitted it for some reason. Readers will probably be aware that, although mortgages are excluded, if a mortgage is other than on a Capital and Interest Repayment basis, the funding vehicle, be it a low-cost endowment policy, PEP or pension, falls within the remit of the FSA and full compliance is required.

At the time of writing a voluntary Code of Practice for Mortgages is being introduced and is mentioned later.

The other products listed above are unregulated because they are basically protection-only products with no investment content. However, many providers of them will only deal with advisers authorised under the FSA. All good advisers wishing to handle these unregulated products will undoubtedly want to adopt an identical stance and to offer best advice, just as if the products were fully regulated; that includes commission disclosure and the reason for the choice of product, the level of cover and general suitability.

Consumer Credit Licence

Under the terms of the Consumer Credit Act 1974 all IFA practices involved in offering credit-related advice to the public, including advice on mortgages, pension loans and re-mortgages, must possess a current Consumer Credit Licence. Referral of clients to other persons also requires registration under the Consumer Credit Act. It is therefore essential that all advisers have a Consumer Credit Licence, whether or not they give advice under the Act.

Advertising

Compliance implications need to be considered in regard to all advertisements, including, but not limited to, letterheads, business cards, compliment slips, facsimile headers, fly-sheets, free sheets, newspaper advertisements, newspaper articles, mailshots and signs or any advertisement through other media. For those working for bank assurers, direct sales organisations, large IFA groups, networks etc there will be in-house rules covering advertising, so the matter is not dealt with extensively here. The main point of which all readers must be aware is that all publications and correspondence with clients and the general public need to be scrutinised and approved for compliance purposes; eg any general mailshot will need specific approval. One major network has an in-house rule that any letter sent to more than 20 separate addresses requires internal approval.

Special business categories

Pension transfers

No reader can be unaware of the pensions mis-selling scandal that was a by-product of easing some PPP regulations from early 1988. All regulators now insist on a higher level of authorisation in this area and many advisers prefer not to become involved. Therefore, if advisers are approached to handle transfers out of final salary schemes, the internal rule book or compliance officer should be consulted as a first step.

Investments in EZPTs, EIS and VCTs

The principles of these schemes are outlined later, but for compliance purposes advisers need to understand the greater risks attached to these investment schemes. A higher level of authorisation may therefore be needed and/or a much stronger risk warning must be issued to and signed by the client; there is a specimen in the Appendices.

Commission disclosure

With effect from 1 January 1995 the entire financial services industry in the UK was required to disclose commission earned on all investment products, life policies and pensions. Disclosure in monetary terms must be made to the client in writing before proposal forms and application forms are signed and submitted. The commission disclosed must be clear and unambiguous and not couched in misleading terms to understate the amounts involved. If renewal commission is payable, that must also be clearly stated, along with whether it is at a flat rate or fund-related.

'Reason why' letters

The present regulations stipulate that 'reason why' letters must be issued to clients entering into long-term financial contracts, generally taken to mean in the narrower sense low-cost endowment policies (supporting a mortgage), personal pension plans or FSAVC contracts. The main purpose of the 'reason why' letter is to confirm the advice given to the client and to explain why that advice is suitable. The explanation should take explicit account of the alternative course of action. It should demonstrate a real link between the circumstances, objectives and risk-profile of the investor and the recommendations made. It should reiterate the main considerations that prompted the advice given. The letter must relate specifically to the particular client. It must not be a photocopy or a standard pro forma letter. However, if a word-processing facility is available it is permissible to store standard paragraphs in software, which can then be selected and incorporated into the 'reason why' letter. The practice has grown in the industry generally of issuing 'reason why' letters for a wider range of investment products than those mentioned above. Some advisers issue a 'reason why' letter with almost every investment recommendation made.

Many advisers, the writer included, prefer to produce a detailed financial report for the client, in which case a 'reason why' letter will not be required, providing the report covers all the relevant points.

A 'reason why' letter should be divided into three sections covering the following:

- An introduction, eg detailing meetings and discussions with the clients, confirming the client's aims and objectives and identifying areas not to be addressed immediately, with a suggested time-scale for review.
- A section detailing generic solutions.
- A section that:
  a identifies the proposed course of action;
  b gives details of the company and product recommended;
  c makes reference to the KFD, which should be enclosed with the 'reason why' letter if it has not already been handed to the client;
  d lists any calculations required to support the advice;

e   asks the investor to get in touch if there is something needing clarification, if further information is required or if the letter does not accord with the investor's view of the position;

f   confirms that the adviser has relied upon information supplied by the investor.

15 Training and Competence

The principal Training and Competence Rules came into effect on 1 October 1995. These rules were introduced to enhance the professional status of all advisers within the industry. The new rules laid down that, for the first time, all advisers must obtain personal authority by passing an examination or, if aged 55 or over, by demonstrating competence by virtue of many years' previous experience. The generally accepted examinations were those for the Financial Planning Certificate (FPC) run by the Chartered Insurance Institute, although various others were accepted, particularly the ACII and ALIA. However, many advisers who had passed those examinations years earlier decided to obtain an FPC on its merits and to ensure that their technical knowledge was up-to-date. After some delay the deadline by which to obtain an FPC was set at 30 June 1997, after which date a significant number of advisers were de-authorised.

At the time of writing around 70,000 advisers hold the FPC or equivalent and many have decided to proceed to obtain an AFPC for a higher qualification, in order to demonstrate professionalism and a commitment to excellence. There are around 3,000 holders of the AFPC at present and that number is expected to grow rapidly. An AFPC qualification entitles the holder to apply for membership of SOFA. There is also a programme to encourage examinations above that level to obtain Associate status and Fellowship status; the Society hopes eventually to achieve its chartered status. There is a view within the industry that the AFPC will become the benchmark qualification. It is too soon to evaluate whether that will happen, but the writer believes that new entrants into the financial services industry who are serious about professionalism and about building a sound career should consider proceeding above the minimum qualifications.

As do most other professional bodies, the industry now requires that practitioners holding the initial qualification undertake continuing professional development (CPD). In relation to financial advisers, this has been defined as '*the planned acquisition, management and development of the technical knowledge, experience and personal skills necessary to give suitable financial advice and carry out professional and technical duties throughout the working life*'. This definition is in line with that adopted by other professional bodies. It is wide in scope and has been developed to emphasise that financial advice is diverse and includes a range of specialists with varying development needs. It encourages many qualifying activities and includes technical updating, business management and administration, personal development and communication skills.

For many, CPD will be a formalisation or extension of their existing professional practice.

Types of CPD

CPD is commonly divided into two categories: structured and unstructured. Structured activity generally involves a third party. It is active and interactive and means that a third party imposes the structure.

Unstructured activity is essentially self-managed; it is not assessed and takes place in a manner appropriate to each individual. In other words, individuals impose their own structures.

CPD activities typically include:

Structured: attendance at conferences, internal training courses, seminars, workshops, technical presentations, annual budget updates and external training courses;

Unstructured: personally reading appropriate professional journals, reports and other financial papers. It does not include reading daily newspapers!

The concept of CPD involves a fair amount of trust being placed in practitioners actually to have done what they claim. So far as structured activity is concerned, authorised course and seminar providers issue CPD certificates as evidence.

At the time of writing, the generally accepted annual commitment to CPD seems to be about 50 hours. Some professional bodies, regulators and compliance departments may specify a longer time which may be split between structured and unstructured. This is a question that will have to be resolved individually according to the working environment. However, the writer is firmly of the opinion that all committed advisers would need to undertake more than 50 hours just to keep pace with the rapid changes within the financial services industry.

The PIA has indicated recently that, in future, all advisers who wish to conduct business in pension transfers must first have passed the Pensions Paper (Code G60) of the AFPC. As well as being allied to the AFPC it is a free-standing qualification. From time to time there are calls within the industry for a new examination to be originated covering precise areas of advice, such as unit trusts, LTCs or even mortgages. These may lead eventually to more examination criteria being imposed and a tightening of the training and competence requirements.

Those wishing to advise on EZPTs, VCTs and EIS can so do, provided they are authorised by their internal regulatory systems. However, the PIA has indicated recently that those advisers wishing to deal in these areas of higher risk should write to the PIA indicating their intention to do so, whereupon it will provide automatic authorisation. The significance will be apparent when those advisers receive PIA monitoring visits. Advisers must keep good CPD records along with the CTP certificate, which will undoubtedly be inspected at monitoring visits. Their internal compliance systems may require that a separate note of all formal training courses be recorded or, alternatively, contained within the CPD records. A specimen CPD record sheet is included in the Appendices.

Individual registration

In February 1998 the PIA introduced a scheme for individual registration. All advisers, directors or partners are required to register, as are managers responsible for activities regulated by the PIA.

Individual registration is not a new concept in the financial services industry. The other SROs and RPBs require certain categories of individual to be registered with them before they may operate. The PIA is adopting a similar approach preparatory to the merger of the three SROs with the other organisations to form the Financial Services Authority. The new regulator has already indicated that it wants to operate individual registration for relevant individuals.

However, there are more intrinsic benefits than merely achieving consistency with the other regulators. The introduction of individual registration should enhance public confidence in the regulatory system. It will demonstrate to investors that the PIA is able to take firm action where necessary, either to prevent an individual from taking up an appointment or to hold him or her accountable for any serious breach of the PIA's rules or the SIB's principles.

In applying to be registered, relevant individuals are applying to enter into a contract with the PIA. Under the terms of that contract they undertake not to cause or assist in causing any PIA-regulated firm to breach any of the PIA's rules or the SIB's principles and agree to comply with those PIA rules relating to them. In March 1998 the PIA sent application forms and guidance notes to all PIA-regulated firms.

The PIA will consider each application on its individual merits. However, as no-one can apply without the support of his or her firm, and as PIA-regulated firms are, or should be, aware of the recruitment standards required, the PIA expects most applicants to accept the contract without question.

Ongoing training and competence

In addition to obtaining initial authorisation and incorporating individual registration and CPD, many larger firms, and probably some smaller ones, have established systems of supervisory control, which means that standards of training and competence are checked constantly and any weaknesses corrected as appropriate

16 Complaints

Overview

At some time most advisers receive complaints from their clients and customers. Complaints should be viewed as the opportunity to demonstrate that, as an adviser, you care about your clients and are able to handle any complaints that may arise.

A complaint is any situation where an individual has expressed dissatisfaction, either orally or in writing, with regard to conduct, service or advice.

All larger organisations have internal complaint-handling procedures but smaller firms may not. The following are sound guidelines to follow when dealing with complainants:

- Do not be defensive, and keep an open mind with regard to the complaint.
- Listen carefully to try to establish the true cause of the complaint.
- Apologise and reassure the client that the complaint will be handled promptly and fairly.
- Immediately make a note in the client's file and in the Complaints Register.
- Implement the complaints procedure if your firm has one.
- Learn from all complaints.

There are strict guidelines laid down by the regulatory authorities as to how complaints relating to insurance and investment business should be handled. For those regulated by the PIA the procedure is set out in Chapter 8 of the PIA Rule Book.

However complaints are made and received, *it is most important that, in addition to the points made above, they are acknowledged immediately in writing, with assurance that the matter will be dealt with swiftly and thoroughly.* All larger IFA practices, members of networks and tied advisers implement internal complaint-handling procedures. In small IFA firms, after the steps set out above have been taken, the principal of the firm should deal with the complaint.

Complaints can be turned to advantage, particularly if they arise as the result of a misunderstanding. The writer remembers receiving a mild complaint some years ago: the client was complaining about a major, highly regarded life office really only because of a lack of communication from them, coupled with lack of general news and of valuations. The client may have received all the paperwork which would normally have been sent out and possibly mislaid it, but was mildly aggravated and inclined to withdraw all funds. The writer took the time to explain gently how well the particular bond had performed, and sent an up-to-date valuation and past performance figures from *Money Management*. The matter was concluded by the client deciding to invest further funds in that particular bond!

Compliance considerations

Monitoring visits by the FSA (or other regulator) or network or other internal audit procedure are certain to look into complaints and how they were handled and resolved, so all advisers should be fully aware of this from the outset. This only reinforces the advice set out above.

17 Advising the Elderly

When dealing with elderly clients there is, perhaps, a more than normal danger of advice not being properly understood. One major bank assurer stipulates that all customers over the age of 70 must be offered the opportunity of being accompanied by a relative or close friend. If the offer is declined, a file note to that effect must be made. All proposed sales to customers over 75 must first be specifically approved by a more senior adviser.

The writer feels that this may be over-defensive. His very old-established firm of solicitors has numerous elderly clients for whom advice has been provided; after seven years no problem has been identified as attributable to advice given to elderly clients. Clearly, additional care should be taken to explain precisely what is recommended and why, and to the writer is another justification for providing written reports that could be produced should difficulties occur, or if advice is queried by, say, an elderly client's children or other professional advisers.

Where a client cannot fully grasp or understand the matter in hand, the additional dangers are obvious and there may well be a need to try and involve a relative or a friend. Once the problem has been identified, any internal procedures should, of course, be followed most carefully. If there are no internal procedures covering the problem it may be desirable to refer the matter to a compliance officer before the recommendation is implemented. An alternative would be to have another adviser present at meetings who could sign a file note confirming that efforts were made to explain suitability.

When advising on long-term care the writer feels it to be absolutely essential that extra steps are taken in the advice-giving process. The writer's firm is a founder member of IFA Care, a voluntary organisation established to promote the provision of long-term care plans in a caring and professional manner by independent financial advisers committed to a specific code of conduct. One of the points of conduct is that all who effect an LTC plan should be told to advise their children (if they have any) of the existence of the plan, or failing that, to advise another professional adviser, their bank manager or a close friend. The reasons for this are obvious. A further point of best practice is that it is highly desirable for a client's children (if any) to be involved in and approve the LTC at the time the contract is entered into.

Home income plans/equity release

Again, when advising elderly clients in these two areas it is highly desirable that a client's children (if any) are made fully aware of the significance of the contract before it is entered into. The writer offers to send copies of quotations, key feature documents and other explanatory material to a client's children if so requested and/or to explain the nature and benefits of the proposed contract at a meeting.

All home income plans are marketed by product providers who are members of Safe Home Income Plans (SHIP). All members of SHIP guarantee security of tenure during the client's lifetime and that of the spouse, and the ability to move house or even to enter sheltered accommodation. Under the scheme no individual plans can be finalised unless the client's solicitors sign a certificate confirming the principal terms of the contract and testifying that it has been fully explained to the client.

Compliance considerations

As well as providing the usual quotations and KFDs, advisers should demonstrate clearly that:

- the additional income to be generated is reasonable in relation to existing income;
- the income tax position is satisfactory;
- the product provider is a member of SHIP;
- reference has been made to the importance of the client's solicitor's certificate;
- the effect of the plan on the elderly client's children or grandchildren (if any) has been fully investigated and understood;
- the elderly client's general state of health has been considered.

18 Share Exchange Schemes and Low-Cost Share Dealing

The writer accepts that many advisers are prohibited from getting involved with this area or, if not prohibited, simply prefer to steer clear of it. However, the fact remains that all advisers are likely to be asked about it at some stage, so a basic knowledge is desirable. Sometimes the two matters are interlinked, as they may present alternatives for dealing with the same problem.

Share exchange schemes

The privatisation programme of the 1980s left many shareholders with small parcels of shares. Indeed there are still thousands of holders of the original flotation of Abbey National shares who received the free offer of 100 shares at issue. The much more recent split of British Gas into BG and Centrica left many holders with a few shares of relatively modest value.

A similar situation can occur on the death of a man (or woman) who enjoyed holding shares but where the surviving spouse has no similar interest and finds the situation unwelcome.

Share exchange schemes were devised some years ago as a way of offering people the chance of exchanging their shares for units in a unit trust, a PEP or a capital investment bond. Conditions of share swaps vary from company to company. Sometimes there will be a charge, but many firms offering the service absorb all the charges themselves. Some groups ask for a minimum total value to make the transaction worthwhile. Often only specific shares will be acceptable; companies tend to favour FTSE 100 stocks and may well refuse to accept shares in small companies, unlisted securities or foreign stocks. This is because some unit trust companies and life offices will only take shares that can be incorporated into those companies' existing portfolios. If the unit trust company or life office does not want to hold the shares, it may refuse to accept them or may pass on the cost of selling to the investor. Share exchange schemes can be of real benefit to the reluctant investor, who can dispose of small holdings at little or no cost and simultaneously move the proceeds into a unit trust or CIB. This spreads the investment risk and enables the choice of a unit trust or life fund that matches current investment aims.

Low-cost share dealing

In the circumstances outlined above, some holders of small parcels of shares may ask advisers how to dispose of them generally or cheaply when they are not interested in share exchange schemes. Most stockbrokers and banks levy a charge on share sales of 1½ per cent, with a minimum of around £30. Therefore, if a person has, say, four such small holdings, each worth a few hundred pounds, the cost of disposal can be relatively high. Taken a stage further, if larger numbers of holdings are involved then possible total savings can be quite significant and worthwhile.

In recent years a number of banks, building societies and stockbrokers, and some 'share shops', have set up low-cost share dealing schemes. These are invariably carried out on an execution-only basis and always by post, except by banks or building societies, where they can be conducted over their counter. Most firms operating a low-cost share dealing service charge 1 per cent on the first £5,000, but subject to a very low minimum – £7.50 to £20. In other words there can be good savings.

The writer keeps a generic file on low-cost share dealing, together with regular press articles on the topic, as well as lists of those who offer this service that appear from time to time in the *Investors Chronicle* and *Which?* magazine.

If clients are adamant that they wish to sell their shares, most advisers should be able to provide help and guidance with little time and trouble and without providing investment advice as such; clients would almost certainly be grateful.

There is a move away from the issue of share certificates and unit trust certificates. Further, the various building societies that demutualised during 1997 now encourage their new shareholders to place their shares in PEPs or share accounts. Both schemes usually include a low-cost share dealing option, so the points made above do not apply and clients should therefore enquire if a cheap share-dealing operation is provided by the demutualised building society.

Another point to note is that some FTSE 100 companies now offer a low-cost share dealing service to their own shareholders, typically at a cost of 1 per cent with a minimum of £10. Therefore, an alternative to approaching providers of low-cost share dealing schemes would be to approach the individual company registrar.

Compliance implications

It seems to the writer that, whatever the level of authorisation, if clients are adamant that they wish to sell shares, an adviser is at liberty to inform them of the existence of low-cost share dealing options. If a client had already decided to re-invest the sale proceeds in an investment product to be arranged by an adviser, and the product provider is able to accept the shares under a share exchange scheme, it seems to the writer that compliance problems are unlikely. The alternative, of course, would be for the shares to be turned into cash and the cash re-invested in the proposed new investment. Provided adequate file notes are made, most compliance procedures would be observed. The point is that advisers must avoid expressing opinions or giving advice as to the merits of selling or not selling the particular shares held.

19 Ethical Investments

Ethical issues are changing our lives – the way we work, what we buy, how we travel – some think that we are experiencing an ethical explosion. From an investor's point of view, there is undoubtedly an increased awareness of ethical investment criteria resulting in a sharp rise in sales of relevant products. In the three years to December 1997 money invested in ethical unit trusts and investment trusts more than doubled to £1.6bn according to the Ethical Research and Information Centre (EIRIS). As a result of this increased awareness, many advisers now incorporate an appropriate question regarding the matter in their Factfind, to raise with new clients, and such a question is included in the writer's Factfind.

What is ethical investment? Arriving at an exact definition is tricky, but broadly speaking it is where ethical considerations influence the choice of investments. A recent survey by EIRIS showed that more than 70 per cent of adults questioned would be influenced by ethical considerations if given a choice of where their money was to be invested. The writer's experience is that very few investors take this view, and, if they do, choice is often limited to the avoidance of alcohol- and tobacco-related companies.

There are currently more than 20 providers offering over 30 ethical funds, comprising unit trusts, investment trusts, PEPs, pensions, FSAVCs, mortgage repayment options and life insurance products. Generally, ethical investment means avoiding investing in companies that generate significant turnover from:

alcohol or tobacco;

export of goods or services for military use;

supplying ozone-depleting chemicals;

testing cosmetics or toiletries on animals;

using intensive farming methods;

extraction/importation of tropical hardwood;

trading in prohibited pesticides;

activities that pollute waterways; and

registered subsidiaries or associates in a significant number of countries identified as violating human rights.

Ethical funds vary in their screening criteria, the sophistication of their ethical 'thinking' and the extent to which they may lobby companies to become more ethical. Some companies, although operating in one or more of the areas listed above, do issue policy statements claiming they operate on a 'green policy' basis, ie they take positive steps not to endanger the environment, by:

careful handling of waste materials;

conserving energy;

avoiding harmful emissions;

reducing noise nuisance;

disposing of containers responsibly.

Running contrary to the above is the view that no public limited company can possibly meet the highest ethical standards because to some extent they all indulge in some unethical practice, or else a subsidiary produces goods that contribute to unethical activities. The banking sector must be a good example. All UK banks clearly do not damage the environment or pollute, but they do finance brewers, chemical companies and farms! Precision engineering companies may manufacture lathes or other capital goods that are then used to manufacture bullets, and mining companies or chemical companies may produce chemicals used in pesticides.

The problems for investors and advisers include the hidden costs of operating ethically. If clients/investors wish ethical considerations to be taken into account, the amount of emphasis to be given in formulating investment plans needs to be determined. The fact that some investment opportunities are excluded may affect overall investment performance.

Ultimately it all depends upon the degree to which the client wishes ethical issues to influence investment decisions.

Effect upon investment performance

For some years there was evidence that ethical investment does not necessarily impede the overall performance of ethical unit trusts and adopting ethical policies therefore should have little impact on total returns. However, it now seems to the writer that there is evidence to the contrary, and those seeking to include ethical considerations in their investment choices are likely to sustain a reduction in overall performance. Some clients may fully accept this, but the writer recommends that the possibility of this should be made very clear, probably in writing.

The following table appeared in the *Daily Telegraph* on 13 December 1997.

How the ethical funds fared					
Fund	£1,000 over five years	Rank	£1,000 over one year	Rank	Fund Size (£ m)
Credit Suisse Fellowship	2,156	1	997	20	71.4
Framlington Health	2,075	2	1,106	4	75.7
Friends Prov Stewardship	1,936	3	1,032	15	300.8
Sovereign Ethical	1,919	4	1,025	17	19.8
TSB Environ Investor	1,904	5	1,125	3	17.8
Scot Equitable Ethical	1,839	6	1,015	18	33.2
United Charities Ethical	1,818	7	1,001	19	7.9
CIS Environ	1,776	8	1,064	10	124.2
Friends Prov Stew Inc	1,733	10	976	21	65.4
Jupiter Ecology	1,709	11	1,048	11	48.8
Allchurches Amity	1,707	12	1,086	7	33.7
Aberdeen Ethical	1,705	13	1,046	12	5.1
Friends Prov Stew N Am	1,692	14	1,172	2	6.3
City Fincl Acorn Ethical	1,672	15	1,076	8	4.8
Abbey Ethical	1,668	16	1,046	13	33.6
Clerical Med Evergreen	1,270	17	1,029	16	19.5
NPI Global Care Income	n/a	n/a	n/a	5	16.2
Henderson Ethical	n/a	n/a	n/a	14	22.9
Equitable Ethical	n/a	n/a	n/a	6	18.0
FPAM Ins Ex Eth UK Equity	n/a	n/a	n/a	1	64.0
Ethical average	*1,785*		*1,063*		
Average for all unit trusts	*2,180*		*1,140*		
FT All Share Index	*2,049*		*1,186*		

Figures are calculated on an offer-to-bid basis with net income reinvested. (Source: Standard and Poor's *Micropal*)

It is outside the scope of this book to cover all aspects of ethical investment. The point of this chapter is to alert readers to the fact that the issues involved may prove to be important to some clients, as well as to provide a basic knowledge of the matter. The writer maintains a generic file on this topic.

Compliance

In the investment report or 'reason why' letter, reference should be made to the client's stated wish for ethical considerations to influence investment recommendations; this should be elaborated in an attempt to quantify the extent or degree of influence. While it will not be difficult to link a client's wishes with an ethical investment recommendation, the possible adverse effects upon overall investment performance should be highlighted.

20 National Savings Products

National Savings products do not pay any commission. Nevertheless, as part of providing suitable advice to clients there will be occasions when National Savings products must be considered, either on a stand-alone basis or as part of a larger portfolio. A major attraction is that as they are backed by the British government they are totally free from investment risk. The attraction of individual products varies periodically in accordance with interest rate and other changes in the investment scene and also according to how keen the government of the day is to raise funds via National Savings.

There is a wide range of products, deliberately designed to appeal to non-taxpayers, basic-rate taxpayers, higher-rate taxpayers and pensioners.

Various products offer:

- a regular monthly income;
- income paid less often;
- income rolled up;
- index-linking;
- tax-free returns.

National Savings has a 'one-stop shop' for financial advisers (telephone 0645 715401) that keeps financial advisers registered with them up to date on National Savings products and interest rate and other product changes.

The lack of commission is disappointing. However, when these products are part of a larger portfolio it may be that the other products used generate an adequate return, and that the inclusion of such non-commission-paying investments can be viewed as a way of 'sharing' commission with a client.

If recommending sole use of a National Savings product, the adviser of course has the usual option of charging a fee. It should be borne in mind, however, that the paperwork is relatively simple, as are the compliance requirements. It may be worth noting here the ease and convenience of dealing with National Savings and the efficiency with which they now respond to financial advisers and the public, providing very quickly over the telephone the latest value of individual holdings of National Savings Certificates. The holders of such certificates are now advised when individual holdings mature and when, if no action is taken, interest will revert to the *general extension rate*, currently 3.51 per cent.

The writer keeps a file on National Savings products, together with copies of application and repayment forms. Useful articles thereon are included from time to time in 'Savings Choice' in the *Daily Telegraph* on Saturdays only.

Compliance

Since all National Savings products are guaranteed by the British government, they are generally considered to be risk-free. There is no inherent investment risk as such, as they are not investment products as defined by the FSA. Therefore, the only compliance issues to be considered and demonstated are the general suitability of the product and that the income tax implications have been borne in mind.

21 Traded Endowment Policies (TEPs)

Overview

Life policies are essentially long-term contracts and it frequently happens that they are discontinued before the full term has expired. The reasons for this are many and varied, eg:

changing circumstances;

sale of a property and no further need for the policy;

inability to maintain premiums;

divorce.

Most such policies are surrendered for whatever the life office offers by way of surrender value. Traditional with-profits life policies cover all charges within the first couple of years, so there are no charges due on surrender after that time. Such policies have a terminal bonus added at maturity which is unlikely to be reflected fully in its surrender value; as a result the policy-holder will lose most or all of the terminal bonus on surrender, as well as the life cover.

As a result the market in TEPs has grown in recent years. That market is not new. Foster & Cranfield have been running auctions in life policies since 1843. However, the market was very small indeed in the years prior to 1978, with only about 150 policies sold per year. The growth came during the 1980s with the introduction of MIRAS and the trend towards funding mortgages by low-cost endowment policies instead of by capital and interest repayment. By the end of the 1980s more than 75 per cent of all new mortgages were arranged on low-cost endowment bases. The recession of the early 1990s hit the housing market very hard and the popularity of low-cost endowments waned. However, the subsequent boom witnessed a huge increase in TEPs.

Attraction to sellers

The growth in the market was driven by the increase in terminal bonuses in the 1980s, and the perceived meanness of some life offices' surrender values. All this resulted in investors buying such policies, continuing to pay the premiums to maturity and then collecting the maturity proceeds including, of course, terminal bonuses. The sellers received additional sums, over and above the surrender values, at no cost whatsoever, and therefore that option, compared with normal surrender, was clearly attractive.

Attraction to buyers/investors

The original policy-holder will have covered all the charges within the first couple of years. With a wide range of policies on the market, buyers can select those that meet their investment needs as regards total outlay, annual premiums and the period to maturity. Indeed, some investors build up portfolios of such policies. UK life offices are generally strong financially and make efforts to maintain their bonuses, although these cannot, of course, be guaranteed; as a result buyers can make a purchase offer for a policy and calculate the likely overall return on their total outlay. That return will be liable either to income tax or to CGT, depending upon whether it is a qualifying or a non-qualifying policy. For such buyers this can represent a sound, low-risk investment opportunity.

How to access this market

There are now numerous players in the second-hand endowment market. Some are auctioneers, but the majority are dealers who simply make cash offers. Most participants are listed in the weekly trade press, *Financial Adviser* and *Money Marketing*. The writer prefers the auction route, using Foster & Cranfield (0171 608 1941). Purchasers of policies have to complete in 28 days. Sellers should receive the sale proceeds within a similar period, but if supporting paperwork is incomplete (eg missing assignments, re-assignments, or birth or marriage certificates) the process will be delayed. Cash offers sometimes proceed more quickly but again progress is dependent upon the vendor (and adviser) ensuring that all paperwork is complete at an early stage. Cash dealers will then sell the policies on as principals to investors.

Remuneration

Foster & Cranfield, acting as auctioneers for a vendor, charge £50 plus one-third of the excess achieved above the surrender value, and out of that third a further division of one-third is payable to advisers or professional investors. As with other auctions, it is possible to stipulate a reserve price.

Most market-makers/dealers pay an introducer's commission of 3 per cent of the value of all policies sold. Other dealers simply make cash offers and leave it to the adviser to charge a fee as the adviser feels appropriate.

It will be seen from the above that the income to be earned from this work is likely to be modest. In the writer's experience it has averaged around £250 per policy.

Practical difficulties

Some market makers/dealers issue leaflets to advisers outlining how easy it is to sell policies in this way, eg simply by obtaining the following:

- the actual policy;
- the surrender value and latest bonus statement;
- birth/marriage certificates if age is not admitted;
- all prior assignments and re-assignments;
- the client's authority to proceed.

The reality is somewhat different. Surrender values have to be obtained or are out-of-date. The latest bonus notices are rarely available and age is rarely admitted. As a result there is usually quite a lot of 'leg work' to be done to collect all the necessary information. The writer would then proceed by asking Foster & Cranfield for an estimate of the likely auction value and obtaining two offers from other dealers before assessing the best way forward.

Likely excess to be obtained above the surrender value

The excess to be achieved is likely to depend upon:

- the standing of the life office and its attraction to investors – linked to the history of its with-profits bonus performance;
- the number of years elapsed and the years left to run;
- the general state of the TEP market at the time.

Generally speaking it seems that the most attractive policies are likely to achieve around 30 per cent above the surrender value, but that can vary considerably both upwards and downwards.

It is most important that readers understand that only traditional with-profits life policies are dealt with in this market. Unit-linked policies and unitised with-profits are simply not tradeable because of the absence of terminal bonuses. The day-to-day values of the units fully reflect the values of the policies.

Compliance

Because a decision to dispose of a life policy is treated as the provision of investment advice, in the same way as the advice to set one up in the first place, it follows that full compliance is required. That means that clients must be advised clearly of the following points in writing, and in effect with a 'reason why' letter:

- The surrender or sale of the policy might not be in their own long-term best interest, as they could be significantly worse off than if they continue to pay the premiums to maturity and collect the terminal bonus.

- They will immediately lose their life cover. If replacement life cover has to be obtained, immediately or in the future, it will almost certainly be more expensive due to increased age and, as the set-up costs for the first policy have been paid, there will be further set-up costs for the replacement policy. In addition, any health problems could lead to a loading on the replacement policy, or even mean (in extreme cases) that obtaining new life cover is impossible.

- Policies issued before 31 March 1984 will have had the benefit of *life policy premium relief*. Briefly, this means that such policies were then subject to a special tax relief of 15 per cent on the premiums, making their return particularly attractive and their premature disposal particularly unattractive.

- To surrender/sell a life policy solely to raise cash, even where the need is great, should be considered carefully. All other options should be examined, including possibly taking a loan on the life policy from the life office concerned, or perhaps obtaining a bank loan if the time to maturity is short.

The following are the broad outlines of acceptable parameters:

1. There is a minimum surrender value of £500 to £1,000.

2. The policy should have been in force for one-quarter of its life, often with a minimum of six years.

3. The shorter the time to maturity the better, but up to 15 years is an acceptable period, subject to 1 and 2 above.

Conclusion

As some policies have little or no appeal to investors, advisers should be most careful initially not to raise their clients' hopes regarding the prospect of a large premium above the stated surrender value.

Another point is that some building societies (with whom the policies are pledged) insist that all proceeds go to reduce the mortgage. While that will, of course, benefit the client, there may be disappointment that both the surrender value and any excess will not go straight into the client's bank account!

22 Venture Capital Trusts (VCTs), Enterprise Investment Scheme (EIS) and Enterprise Zone Property Trusts (EZPTs)

These three higher-risk investment schemes are briefly examined together. Most readers will not become involved with them because of the limited range of products on which they are able to advise or because of their firm's internal restrictions, and because all have limited appeal to the investing public. However, all advisers should be aware of them because they may be attractive to certain types of investor in certain circumstances:

- those who like to take higher risks;
- higher-rate taxpayers;
- those with substantial CGT liabilities;
- investors who really can understand the risks and are attracted to a particular scheme.

Venture Capital Trusts

VCTs are quoted investment companies that invest their shareholders' funds in private companies or companies quoted on the Alternative Investment Market (AIM). There are four basic tax breaks available to a VCT investor, who may place up to £100,000 therein in any one tax year:

1. Dividends on ordinary shares in the trusts are exempt from income tax.
2. Subscribers to new VCT shares are entitled to 20 per cent income tax relief provided the shares are held for at least five years, ie an investment of £80 would be worth £100 of VCT shares.
3. Investors are exempt from CGT on the sale of ordinary shares, and new subscribers may also use a VCT scheme to defer an existing CGT liability, up to the amount subscribed. Only the gain needs to be invested, not the total sale proceeds of the investment that generated the CGT liability.

There is usually a spate of new VCT schemes in February and March each year as the tax year-end approaches and potential investors effect year-end tax-planning. It is probably advisable to regard VCTs as a specialised investment vehicle with attractive tax features, rather than solely as a tax-planning tool. Investors interested in venture capital should also be aware that there are other vehicles available giving exposure to that sector.

As the first VCT schemes were launched only in 1995 it is too soon for any general pattern of investment success to have emerged. The initial growth of VCT shares has been modest, but if investment managers get it right and investment conditions are favourable there could well be very high returns within a couple of years.

Enterprise Investment Scheme

The EIS was announced in the November 1993 Budget as a simplified replacement for the Business Expansion Scheme (BES), which was withdrawn. The EIS came into force on 1 January 1994. In the March 1998 Budget the EIS was merged with the CGT Reinvestment Relief. The revised EIS is aimed at encouraging investment in new shares in qualifying trading companies. The main changes are:

- an increase of 50 per cent per annum in the amount that can be invested, up to £150,000;
- unlimited deferral relief from CGT for individuals and trustees where disposals are invested in eligible shares;
- when EIS shares are issued in the first half of the tax year the tax relief can be carried back to the preceding year, subject to 50 per cent of the amount subscribed, to a maximum of £25,000;
- extension of the limitation on the underlying investment by the exclusion of farming, forestry, property, hotels and nursing home companies.

The EIS comprises a series of tax reliefs which are available to qualifying new equity investments in qualifying unquoted companies. The principal reliefs are:

- initial tax relief of 20 per cent of the amount subscribed;
- deferment of CGT due;
- exemption from CGT, provided the investment is held for five years.

The pitfalls include a combination of higher risk and absence of liquidity, coupled with uncertainty about the final exit route after five years. EIS investments perhaps should be compared with a VCT, ie as a quoted company, which should mean that the shares are readily saleable.

Enterprise Zone Property Trusts

Enterprise Zones were first established in 1981 to facilitate economic regeneration in areas targeted for commercial activity. To attract private-sector investment, initial tax allowances of 100 per cent are given on commercial property development in Enterprise Zones. The zones themselves benefit from a simplified planning regime and occupiers enjoy exemption from non-domestic business rates.

An Enterprise Zone Property Trust acquires commercial property on behalf of investors. Investors, in turn, acquire units in the EZPT and are entitled to tax allowances pro rata for the value of the units acquired. There is no limit to the amount that may be invested in an EZPT. It is only the size of each EZPT that ultimately restricts availability and, accordingly, most investors can normally select the number of units to match exactly their requirements for tax relief. Another feature of EZPTs is that, typically, loans are made available to enable investors to structure their investments in a more tax-efficient manner with immediate cashflow benefits.

EZPTs invest in offices, industrial and, to a lesser extent, retail property within Enterprise Zones. These properties may be pre-let or speculative. In pre-let properties long-term tenants will have been identified prior to acquisition by the EZPT. As a result investors often receive rental income from the property immediately.

EZPTs can provide investors with a means of investing directly into commercial property while sheltering unlimited levels of income at the highest marginal rate of tax. Investment in EZPTs can be structured in such a way that no net cash outlay is required because, in addition to obtaining tax relief, investors are typically offered a finance facility of up to 70 per cent of the cost of the investment via a pre-packaged loan. In other words, the tax rebate is greater than the net investment.

EZPTs are designed as long-term investments and, in order for the tax reliefs to be safeguarded, the trust must remain in existence for 25 years. However, after seven years what is called a 'lesser interest' in the property can be sold. The amount that can be invested is unlimited; however, there is usually a minimum investment requirement of £5,000, or £22,000 if a loan facility is used. The tax relief available under the EZPT scheme is quite independent of other tax incentives such as the VCT scheme or the EIS.

The investment risks are hard to quantify. The ultimate success of the investment will depend upon the growth and future price levels of the underlying properties, which can be subject to price distortion because of the accruing tax allowances. Even ignoring that, there may well be wide fluctuations in prices as a result of the degree of success or otherwise of each individual Enterprise Zone. EZPT investments are intended to be held for long periods, usually 25 years, and there is no established market in which to trade them. If the underlying property is realised within seven years, there will be a clawback of the capital allowances.

It is the writer's personal opinion that EZPT investment should be entered into only by those with some knowledge of commercial property and who are able to evaluate the underlying investment risks for themselves.

Conclusion and compliance

The complex nature of these three schemes will be apparent. Advisers asked to investigate and possibly recommend one of them should first check with their compliance department. If the decision is to proceed, the following action is recommended:

1. Quantify the tax breaks – both the initial income tax benefits and the possible deferment of CGT.

2. Ensure the client fully accepts that the funds are totally committed for the stated period and that even after that time realisation may be difficult.

3. Try to quantify the investment risk. In 1997 the writer suggested that a wealthy client defer a CGT liability by the purchase of shares in a local, well-known but privately owned brewery. The investment risk was not perceived to be very great. The matter did not proceed because the shares were sold elsewhere. Later the same client considered a VCT scheme: investing in one or more sea-going vessels which would service oilrigs in the North Sea. The ultimate success of this latter venture really depended upon the resale value of the vessel(s). Here the risks seemed to be very much greater and the client did not proceed.

4. A special risk warning should be signed, a specimen of which is included in the Appendices.

It seems to the writer that these three schemes can have very substantial tax benefits but should be entered only into by experienced investors, and advisers should proceed with care!

23 Mortgage Advice

Overview

Readers who have arranged mortgages for themselves recently will know how very complex the matter has become. Mortgages are not controlled by the FSA, but a repayment vehicle may be if it is regulated, ie:

- a PEP or, in future, an ISA;
- an endowment policy;
- a pension policy.

It therefore follows that only capital and interest repayment mortgages and interest-only mortgages are totally unregulated by the Financial Services Act.

Indeed, for many years the only choice on effecting a mortgage was either capital and interest repayment or the low-cost endowment route. Both types were usually linked to a variable interest rate.

Then the market changed. In the early 1980s all the big banks entered the mortgage market for the first time and centralised lenders appeared. Both types of entrant spawned a proliferation of more complex mortgage schemes:

- fixed-rate mortgages;
- capped/collared rates;
- discounts off the variable rate;
- cashbacks;
- stabilised payment schemes.

Matters then became more complex by a combination of some of the above products being offered in the mortgage marketplace. Fixed rates were generally set for a couple of years but were then extended for (currently) up to ten years, and discounts off variable rates produced a further range of options:

- a very large discount for a short period;
- a lesser discount for a longer period;
- lower discounts coupled with the absence of early redemption penalties.

The mortgage 'package' then became even harder for the public and advisers to evaluate and compare, because of:

- the inclusion (or not) of compulsory insurances;
- the impact of the Mortgage Indemnity Guarantee (MIG) and its costs, varying considerably between lenders, together with the ability to add the cost of the MIG to the loan;
- loyalty bonuses, re-mortgage offers, offers to pay legal fees, offers of free surveys etc;
- different methods of calculating interest.

All these developments resulted in immense complexity. Indeed, the headline mortgage rate may well not be quite what it seems and so the provision of sound advice in this area is complicated. The writer knows of numerous advisers who now prefer not to offer mortgage advice at all or, if they do, to charge fees.

The writer's policy is to charge an initial fee of £150 for the provision of a comprehensive range of mortgage advice, including quotations. The fee is payable whether or not the mortgage proceeds; if it does, the fee is refunded in full and the writer's firm receives whatever fee, if any, the lender pays, as well as any commission that may be payable on insurance policies used to support the mortgage.

Keeping up to date on mortgages and providing best advice

This can be achieved by a combination of:

1. regularly noting and filing the weekend 'best buy' tables in national newspapers;
2. researching more detailed 'best buy' tables which appear regularly in trade papers;
3. joining mailing lists for good lenders' products;
4. using computer-based mortgage source data; this is provided at varying cost usually by centralised lenders or other intermediaries.

The time it takes to keep up to date on a daily basis is now very onerous, and is a further reason for some advisers preferring not to become involved. Some larger IFA firms have advisers specialising in mortgages, and bank assurers, because of their size, find it convenient to have dedicated 'mortgage counsellors' in their branches. Of course, these mortgage counsellors can advise only on their own company's products.

Mortgage 'wholesalers' or 'packagers'

These firms typically act as the 'intermediary's intermediary'. This means that they distribute products from a panel of lenders, sometimes developing exclusive products not attainable through other sources for intermediaries who use their services.

If they also 'package', they may undertake some of the work that the lender would otherwise do in-house, such as gathering information about the borrower to enable the lender to check the borrower's status.

There can be distinct advantages for a financial adviser to use such wholesalers:

- they usually pay fees to introducers, typically £150;
- they tend to have good, fast administration;
- they sometimes use generic application forms which can be passed to more than one lender on the panel, thereby precluding the applicant from having to complete a second application form later;
- from time to time some have (in the writer's experience) outstandingly good mortgage package offers available.

Best advice on mortgages

This is a difficult area and needs to be broken down into two distinct parts:

1. The structure of the mortgage itself:
   - fixed or variable interest rate;
   - if fixed, for how long;
   - length of discount off variable rate;
   - penalty period;
   - 'strings' attached.
2. How the mortgage is to be repaid.

The writer finds the second point easier to resolve and always tackles that first. Low-cost endowments have had a very bad press in recent years, somewhat unfairly in the writer's view. While pension mortgages can have tax advantages for the higher paid, the writer is uneasy about linking a client's pension plans to mortgage arrangements because any unexpected change in the borrower's circumstances may mean that trying to alter one may impact adversely on the other.

The writer strongly favoured PEP mortgages, but only for those clients able to fully understand and accept the concept. ISAs will be available after April 1999 but the tax benefits are less. As a result many more people now are choosing the capital and interest repayment method, which is, of course, much easier to advise upon.

Once the funding arrangement is resolved, the matter of how the mortgage is to be structured can be tackled. The two main options are fixed rate or variable rate. Generally speaking the choice will come down to personal preference, together with the borrower's (and the adviser's) view of the likely trend in interest rates.

As a general rule fixed-rate mortgages are likely to be more attractive to borrowers who are taking on a maximum commitment and for whom a significant increase in the mortgage rate would jeopardise their personal or family finances. If the proposed mortgage commitment is much less onerous then, at the time of writing at least, the discount off the variable rate may well offer a more attractive and cost-saving alternative. There are snags to fixed-rate mortgages:

- There is always a fee payable.
- There are penalties for early redemption and such penalties may well extend beyond the period of the fixed rate. However, the mortgage may well be portable.
- If interest rates drop the fixed rate may soon look unattractive.

Variable-rate mortgages rarely carry arrangement fees but, as mentioned, generally carry penalty periods extending beyond the period of the variable-rate discount. The borrower personally takes the risk as to the future level of interest rates.

Having resolved how the mortgage is to be constructed, the borrower and adviser need to consider which company will provide the mortgage, as well as considering the following.

- compulsory insurances or the absence of them;
- whether or not a MIG is payable and, if so, at what rate;
- any cash offers available towards legal fees and/or survey fees;
- possible free surveys;
- penalty periods and portability;
- the lender's overall rating in the mortgage market and the history of charging rates above/below the market average, as that may well apply to a fixed-rate mortgage once the fixed-rate period has expired.

Readers who have not yet attempted to arrange a mortgage or to advise on one may find the idea either depressing or a challenge! But be warned; to give good, sound mortgage advice is very time-consuming indeed.

The Mortgage Code

The new Financial Regulatory Reform Bill, to be introduced in late 1998, will include provision for the Treasury to extend the scope of the Financial Services Act to include mortgages if it chooses.

The industry is now officially on trial and, if the government decides the Council of Mortgage Lenders' Code of Practice has failed, it will be able to move swiftly to statutory regulation. Lenders have until mid-1999, when the government will then undertake its first formal investigation into how the Code is working. This means that the Code for lenders will have been in place for two years and for intermediaries for one year. This gives more breathing space than some companies had expected. The Code will be judged on its effectiveness in ensuring that good advice is given to borrowers, and on how well it remedies borrowers' grievances.

From 30 April 1998 the Council of Mortgage Lenders' Code, to which virtually all lenders subscribe, requires that mortgage brokers register with the Mortgage Code Registry of Intermediaries (MCRI) or face being banned from doing business with lenders who have signed up to the Code. The Code bans CML lenders from offering home loans through unregistered brokers, and intermediaries are obliged to comply, but the Code will remain voluntary and is less than perfect. Many details have still to be finalised. Key elements of the Mortgage Code are set out in the Appendices.

Problem mortgages

All banks, building societies and other high-street lenders are very reluctant to grant mortgages to people who have histories involving:

- mortgage arrears, however small;
- county court judgments;
- other previous credit problems;
- bankruptcy/insolvency;
- insufficient records or accounts (eg the self-employed).

As a result there is now a range of lenders sometimes willing to grant mortgages to people the high street lenders have declined. Most of these lenders charge either very high arrangement fees, or very high interest rates, or a combination of both. While people in those circumstances obviously need help, and may therefore be willing to pay high fees or high interest rates, advisers should proceed with care.

Compliance

Compliance is now in accordance with the Mortgage Code rather than with the Financial Services Act. Compliance with the Mortgage Code clearly means that the files must demonstrate the research carried out and the reason for specific mortgages being recommended, together with demonstration of best advice.

The borrower's attitude to the risk attached to a variable-rate mortgage, compared with a fixed rate moving against them, will need to be properly recorded, coupled with the relative attraction of the absence of compulsory insurance and the inclusion of cashbacks or other incentives. If an adviser manages to arrange a 'problem mortgage' at high rates or carrying high fees, then the facts will need to be properly recorded on the file and, in the writer's personal opinion, the borrower should sign a declaration confirming an understanding of why these exceptional costs have had to be incurred.

24 Conclusion

To be successful a financial adviser needs to have real interest and enthusiasm, but existing and potential advisers should remember that from their clients' perspective buying or arranging an investment product is rarely an enjoyable experience! Many clients will be unable or unwilling to grasp fully all the implications of the protection product or investment product to which they have agreed.

Even in the fullness of time some clients will still not realise just how well a good investment has performed and what it has achieved for them, let alone have the ability to compare it with any alternatives considered at the outset. On the other hand many will realise how well they have been served and that, as a result, they are much better off or have the benefit of having the right protection product in place.

Successful advisers can gain vast personal and job satisfaction in the knowledge that their skills and judgment have benefited their clients on a lasting basis.

Appendix I: Specimen Factfind

CLIENT FINANCIAL INFORMATION

NAME

PARTNER

The LIFA **ASSOCIATION**

SECTION 1: What Are Your Financial Goals? *Please tick appropriate boxes below:*

	Yes	No
Providing for your family in the event of death	❏	❏
Providing for your family in the event of permanent ill health	❏	❏
Providing for your family in the event of a critical illness	❏	❏
Providing for medical expenses	❏	❏
Buying or improving a house or repaying your mortgage	❏	❏
Raising money	❏	❏
Planning your retirement	❏	❏
Savings for a specific purpose	❏	❏
Providing for school fees	❏	❏
Producing a good return on your savings	❏	❏
Increasing your income	❏	❏
Investing a lump sum	❏	❏
Reducing your tax bill	❏	❏
Mitigating Inheritance Tax	❏	❏

Over what period are you prepared to invest for?   Short 1-5 yrs) ❏   Medium (6-15 yrs) ❏   Long (15+ yrs) ❏

How speculative are you prepared to be when considering investments?

Little risk / very speculative

In relation to the type of product:

1	2	3	4	5	6	7	8	9	10

In relation to the fund invested in:

1	2	3	4	5	6	7	8	9	10

Do you have strong views on where your money is invested?

Any other matter - please give details (additional space is provided in Section 9)

SECTION 2: Personal Details

	SELF	PARTNER
Address		Address if different
Contact phone number	day	day
	night	night
Date of birth		
Marital status		
National Insurance Number		
Are you in good health	Yes/ No	Yes/ No
Smoker	Yes/ No	Yes/ No
Dependants		
Dependants ages or dates of birth		
Dependants relationship		
Have you made a will	Yes/ No	Yes/ No

What are the main provisions of the will (additional space is given in Section 9)		
Have you received or made any gifts which may affect inheritance tax liabilities -please give details	£ £ £	£ £ £

SECTION 3: *Employment And Income*

Employment Status				
Employer occupation				
Position				
Length of service				
Gross annual salary	£	per annum	£	per annum
Benefits in kind	£	per annum	£	per annum
Net basic salary	£	per mth	£	per mth
Bonus/commission/overtime	£	per mth	£	per mth
Unearned Income	£	per mth	£	per mth
Total net income	£	per mth	£	per mth
Maximum rate of tax	%		%	
Tax Reference and district				
Are you in a company pension	Yes/ No		Yes/ No	
Is there a company pension	Yes/ No		Yes/ No	
Eligibility conditions to join				
Employer's contribution	%		%	
Employee's contribution	%		%	
Basis of scheme and eligibility				
AVC/FSAVC				
Desired retirement age	yrs		yrs	
Anticipated changes				

SECTION 4: *Personal Liabilities and Expenditure*

Mortage/ rent	£	per mth	£	per mth
Loans/cards outstanding				
(total)	£		£	
Monthly payment	£	per mth	£	per mth
Other liabilities:				
outstanding	£		£	
	£		£	
Monthly commitment	£	per mth	£	per mth
	£	per mth	£	per mth
Total monthly outgoings	£	per mth	£	per mth
Surplus income	£	per mth	£	per mth

SECTION 5: Home

Home	£	£
Mortgage outstanding	£	£
What type of mortgage is it		
When is the repayment date		
Second property (if any)	£	£
How is this/ these owned	Sole tenancy/Tenants in common/joint tenancy	

Do you have vacant possession of this/either property

	Yes/ No	Yes/ No
Do you have any CCJs or arrears	Yes/ No	Yes/ No
House contents and other personal effects	£	£

SECTION 6: Other Assets

Product	Provider	Premium	Lump sum or regular premium	Value- Self	Value- Partner
Cash savings / MIPs				£	£
				£	£
Unit trusts				£	£
				£	£
PEPs				£	£
				£	£
Bonds				£	£
				£	£
TESSAs				£	£
				£	£
Shares - quoted				£	£
				£	£
Shares - unquoted				£	£
				£	£
National Savings				£	£
				£	£
Other (specify)				£	£
				£	£

SECTION 7: Pension Arrangements

Type of pension -occupational/personal	Life office	Retirement age	Estimated pension benefits	Death in service benefits	Beneficiary	Personal contribution	Value
Self (specify type)						£	£
						£	£
Partner (specify type)						£	£
						£	£

CLIENT FINANCIAL INFORMATION

SECTION 8: *Life Assurance And Protection Arrangements*

Type of policy/ protection	Life office	Maturity/ expiry date	Sum assured	Premium	Other benefits	Is policy under trust	Beneficiary	Value -Self	Value -Partner
Life - specify type								£	£
								£	£
								£	£
								£	£
PHI					£			£	£
PMI					£				
Critical Illness					£			£	£
Other (specify)								£	£
								£	£

SECTION 9: *Further Information*

Are you a professional ❑ business ❑ or experienced ❑ investor *(tick any box which applies)*

SECTION 10: *Sundry Requirements And Notes*

Purpose	Capital/Income/Both/Other (specify)
Required benefits (specify)	
Accessibility of funds in the event of emergency	Immediate/Less than one month/Less than three months/Other (specify)
Deferment periods	wks
Waiver of premiums	Yes/No
Lives assured	
Hazardous sports	Yes/No
Other (specify)	

Declaration
This information has been provided on the understanding that it will be used in strict confidence and that it places us under no obligation to take up any suggested recommendation

Signature of self

Date

Signature of partner

Date

98

SECTION 11: *Consultants Notes*

SECTION 12: *Needs Identified*

Product	Reason why
Company	Reason why
Product	Reason why
Company	Reason why
Product	Reason why
Company	Reason why

Appendix 2: Specimen Clients' Information Sheet (IFA)

Crossley Morris Financial Services

Terms and Conditions of Business

Crossley Morris Financial Services are independent advisers, being regulated by the Personal Investment Authority.

Regulator's statement

Those who advise on life assurance, pensions or unit trusts are

EITHER   independent advisers

OR   representatives of one company

Crossley Morris Financial Services are independent and will act on your behalf in advising you on life assurance, pensions or unit trust products. Because we are independent we can advise you on the products of different companies. We are bound by the PIA (Personal Investment Authority) Rules.

We hope the following will assist you in understanding the services which we aim to provide.

Independent financial advice

We offer independent financial advice but occasions can arise where we, or one of our other customers, will have some form of interest in business which we are transacting for you. If this happens, or we become aware that our interests or those of one of our other customers conflict with your interests, we will inform you and obtain your consent before we carry out your instructions.

When we have arranged any investments for you for which you have given instructions, in response to our enclosed recommendations, we will not give you any further advice unless you request it but will be glad to advise you at any time you ask us to do so.

We require our clients to give us instructions in writing, to avoid possible disputes. We will, however, accept oral instructions providing they are subsequently confirmed in writing. You, or we, may terminate our authority to act on your behalf at any time, without penalty. Notice of this termination must be given in writing.

Commissions

We derive income from commissions paid to us by life assurance companies and unit trust managers with which investments are made. You will receive from the Life Office, or from us, information about the commission that we receive. We shall tell you the amount of commission payable to us on any such investment. If we arrange for you to take out a life policy, we will not normally charge you a fee for our services because we will receive commission from the life insurance company or friendly society.

If you subsequently cease to pay premiums on the Policy and in consequence we are obliged to refund the commission that has been paid to us we reserve the right to charge you a fee based on the number of hours spend in advising you and arranging the policy. We will not charge any fee if you exercise your right to cancel the policy in accordance with the cancellation notice sent to you by the life assurance company or friendly society.

If we recommend to you any policy to which this paragraph applies, we will, at the same time, inform you in writing of the maximum amount of any such fee and of the latest time at which we would charge it.

Charges

Whilst we do not normally charge fees, we will do so at an hourly agreed rate if the work we do for you does not relate to investments on which commission is payable. In addition, fees may be payable where you instruct us to give you advice but not to arrange a sale or purchase of any investment product for you. Where we propose to charge a fee, we will notify you, in writing, before we carry out any chargeable work, explaining how it will be calculated, or how much it will be.

Records

We keep records of all your investment transactions for up to seven years. You have the right to inspect the records at a convenient time.

Professional indemnity insurance

We confirm that we maintain adequate professional indemnity insurance for your protection in the event of our negligence. Details of this insurance, including the current limits of indemnity, are available on request.

Complaints

If you should have any complaint about the advice you receive or a product which you have bought, please write to Grahame Crossley, Crossley Morris Financial Services, 19–21 Halliwell Street, Chorley, PR7 2AL. Telephone: (01257) 260311. Crossley Morris Financial Services has only one Partner who is engaged in the day to day conduct of investment business. If he were unable to conduct business (say through illness) then Crossley Morris Financial Services would not want your interests to suffer. We have, therefore, made a formal arrangement with Abrams Ashton Chartered Accountants, 41 St Thomas' Road, Chorley, Lancashire PR7 1JE, Telephone (01257) 273313, to carry out our investment business obligations if we were unable to conduct investment business for more than fourteen days.

Compensation scheme for investors

If you make a valid claim against Crossley Morris Financial Services in respect of the investments we arrange for you and we are unable to meet our liabilities in full, you may be entitled to redress from the Investors Compensation Scheme. Details of the cover provided by the Scheme are given in a leaflet which we will send you at your request.

WE HAVE NOT SOUGHT AUTHORISATION FROM THE PERSONAL INVESTMENT AUTHORITY TO HANDLE CLIENTS' MONEY AND WE NEVER ACCEPT A CHEQUE MADE PAYABLE TO OURSELVES (UNLESS IT IS A CHEQUE IN SETTLEMENT OF CHARGES OR DISBURSEMENTS FOR WHICH WE HAVE SENT YOU AN INVOICE) OR HANDLE CASH. ALL CHEQUES MUST BE MADE PAYABLE TO THE INSURANCE COMPANY OR UNIT TRUST GROUP OR ALTERNATIVELY, INVESTMENTS MUST BE MADE BY DIRECT DEBIT OR BANKER'S ORDER.

Signed .... Crossley Morris Financial Services
19–21 Halliwell Street
Chorley
Lancashire
PR7 2AL
Tel: (01257) 260311

I.. sign and return this copy of the Terms of Business confirming that I am agreeable to you acting as my independent financial adviser.

Signature ....

Signature ....
(partner if applicable)

Appendix 3: Specimen Clients' Information Sheet

Midland Bank

TERMS OF BUSINESS LETTER

This is an important document which you should keep for future reference. It explains the services we offer and what your rights are. The following statement provided by our regulator, the Personal Investment Authority, explains the status of our financial advisers and the nature of the advice they can give you.

> *Regulator's Statement*
>
> *Those who advise on life assurance, pensions or unit trust products are*
>
> > *EITHER: representatives of one company*
> > *OR: independent advisers*
>
> *Your adviser represents Midland Bank plc and acts on its behalf. Midland Bank plc is part of the Midland marketing group. Your adviser can only give you advice on the life assurance, pensions and unit trust products of the Midland marketing group. Because your adviser is not independent he or she cannot advise you on the purchase of products of this type available from providers other than those of the Midland marketing group.*

The services we offer:

- Midland Bank plc is a principal member of the HSBC Group*, one of the world's largest banking and financial services organisations. We aim to offer you value for money products and quality service.

- We offer advice and guidance on a wide range of products including life assurance, pensions, Personal Equity Plans and unit trusts. Our Financial Planning Managers and Financial Planning Officers are trained professionals you can trust to help you make an informed decision about your financial future.

- If you have any queries relating to this document or our products, please do not hesitate to contact your Financial Planning Manager or Financial Planning Officer.

We aim to:

- Establish and understand your current and future needs through a confidential discussion of your financial circumstances.

- Make recommendations based upon the information provided by you.

- Explain clearly the reasons for our recommendations, the benefits, and the commitment required from you for any products we recommend.

- Help you to review your financial arrangements in the future to ensure they continue to meet your changing needs.

- Keep you up to date on how your Midland plans are doing and give you information which you may find useful.

The advice you receive:

- We take full responsibility for the advice we give to you. Should you have any complaint about the advice you receive or a product you have bought, contact your Financial Planning Manager or Financial Planning Officer and we will ensure that it is dealt with quickly and efficiently.

- If you are unable to resolve your complaint through your Financial Planning Manager or Financial Planning Officer, please write to: The Customer Relations Manager, Midland Personal Financial Services, Norwich House, Nelson Gate, Commercial Road, Southampton, SO15 1GX or telephone 01703 229929.

- If you make a valid claim against Midland in respect of the investments we arrange for you and we are unable to meet our liabilities in full, you may be entitled to redress from the Investors Compensation Scheme. Details of the cover provided by the Scheme are given in a leaflet. Should you wish to receive a copy of this leaflet, please contact the Compliance Officer, Midland Compliance, Midland Bank plc, 27-32 Poultry, London, EC2P 2BX.

- Midland Bank plc is regulated by the Personal Investment Authority and is bound by the Personal Investment Authority's rules.

Your access to records:

- You have the right to inspect copies of contract notes, vouchers and entries in our books, or computerised records relating to your transactions. Records are kept for at least six years.

Personal Data:

- The details you provide will be held on our computer records.

- We may share information about you and the conduct of your account with:
  - other members of the HSBC Group*:- to provide you with the service applied for; to assist in servicing your other relationships with the HSBC Group*; in making lending decisions; for fraud prevention; audit purposes; or debt collection.
  - other third parties:- to provide you with the service applied for; to help resolve a complaint; for fraud prevention; audit purposes; debt collection; or so that services may be processed on our behalf.

- We may send you information about products and services of the HSBC Group* which we feel may interest you. If you would prefer not to receive these details, please write to your local Midland branch.

- To help improve our service and in the interest of security, we may monitor and/or record your telephone calls with us.

*The HSBC Group means HSBC Holdings plc, its subsidiaries and associated companies.

Midland Bank plc
Poultry, London EC2P 2BX
Telephone: 0171-260 8190

20359-9 (03/98- UOI=1 x FK100) 34/5

Member HSBC *Group*

Appendix 4: Standard Inflation Table

The following table shows what £1,000 will be worth in today's money at the end of the period shown and at the annual rates of inflation given.

Period (Years)	Rate of Inflation		
	4%	7%	10%
	£	£	£
5	822	713	621
10	676	508	386
15	555	362	239
20	456	258	149
25	375	184	92
30	308	131	57
35	253	94	36
40	208	67	22
45	171	48	14
50	141	34	9

Appendix 5: CGT Indexation Table

How to calculate your capital gains

This table is designed to help you calculate how much of any capital gain may be attributed to inflation and so can be deducted from liability to tax.

For example, if shares were bought in March 1982 for £1,000 and sold in February 1998 – the latest date for which official inflation figures are currently available – the original purchase price should be multiplied by the March 1982 indexation factor of 2.018.

So, in this case, £2,018 can be deducted from the sale price in calculating the chargeable gain.

Where the sale of assets occurred before February 1998, you can arrive at the correct indexation factor by dividing the figure shown for the month of acquisition by the figure for the month of sale. Then use the resulting figure to multiply the original cost and deduct the total from the sale proceeds.

Everyone is entitled to take gains of £6,500 this year without becoming liable to capital gains tax, and so married couples can raise gains of £13,000 without needing to pay this tax. Since 29 November 1993, the allowance cannot create or increase an allowable loss but would apply to the costs of purchase.

Indexation applies separately to each item of original cost – reduced as necessary by holdover or rollover relief – and improvement expenditure. In each case, indexation runs from the date the expenditure was incurred. Indexation does not apply to allowable sale costs, such as professional fees and valuation. For monthly savings schemes in unit trusts and investment trusts, where there are fixed monthly savings and no more than small withdrawals, the whole investment for the year – monthly savings less any small withdrawals – can be treated, for the purposes of calculating the indexation factor, as if it were made in the seventh month of the trust's accounts.

So, if the trust has a 31 December year-end, the seventh month is July.

Indexation Allowance: February 1998

The value of the retail prices index, as published by the Office for National Statistics, for February 1998 is 160.3 (January 1987=100). The indexed rise to be used in calculating the indexation allowance in respect of assets disposed of in February 1998 is as follows:

	1982	1983	1984	1985	1986	1987	1988	1989	1990	1991	1992	1993	1994	1995	1996	1997	1998
Jan	–	1.940	1.846	1.758	1.665	1.603	1.552	1.444	1.341	1.231	1.182	1.162	1.134	1.098	1.067	1.038	1.005
Feb	–	1.932	1.838	1.744	1.659	1.597	1.546	1.434	1.334	1.225	1.176	1.155	1.128	1.091	1.062	1.034	–
Mar	2.018	1.929	1.832	1.727	1.657	1.593	1.540	1.427	1.320	1.220	1.173	1.151	1.125	1.087	1.058	1.032	–
Apr	1.978	1.902	1.808	1.691	1.641	1.575	1.515	1.402	1.281	1.204	1.155	1.140	1.112	1.076	1.050	1.026	–
May	1.964	1.894	1.802	1.684	1.638	1.573	1.509	1.394	1.270	1.201	1.151	1.136	1.108	1.072	1.048	1.022	–
Jun	1.958	1.889	1.797	1.680	1.639	1.573	1.504	1.389	1.265	1.195	1.151	1.137	1.108	1.070	1.048	1.018	–
Jul	1.958	1.879	1.799	1.683	1.644	1.575	1.502	1.388	1.264	1.198	1.155	1.139	1.113	1.075	1.052	1.018	–
Aug	1.957	1.871	1.782	1.679	1.639	1.570	1.486	1.384	1.251	1.195	1.154	1.134	1.108	1.069	1.047	1.011	–
Sep	1.958	1.863	1.779	1.680	1.631	1.565	1.479	1.375	1.240	1.191	1.150	1.130	1.106	1.064	1.042	1.006	–
Oct	1.949	1.856	1.768	1.677	1.628	1.558	1.464	1.364	1.230	1.187	1.146	1.130	1.104	1.070	1.042	1.005	–
Nov	1.939	1.850	1.762	1.671	1.614	1.550	1.457	1.353	1.233	1.182	1.147	1.132	1.103	1.070	1.042	1.004	–
Dec	1.943	1.845	1.764	1.669	1.609	1.552	1.453	1.349	1.234	1.181	1.152	1.130	1.098	1.064	1.038	1.002	–

The RI month for disposals by individuals on or after 6 April 1985 (1 April 1985 for companies) is the month in which the allowable expenditure was incurred, or March 1982 where the expenditure was incurred before that month.

Appendix 6: Mortality Tables

Life expectation

(Taken from tables produced by the Government Actuary's Department)
Mean expectation of life, expressed in years, based on data for 1991–93.

Age	Males	Females	Age	Males	Females
0	73.67	79.09	29	46.00	51.00
1	73.23	78.55	30	45.04	50.02
2	72.27	77.59	31	44.08	49.04
3	71.30	76.62	32	43.13	48.06
4	70.32	75.63	33	42.17	47.09
5	69.33	74.64	34	41.21	46.11
6	68.35	73.66	35	40.25	45.14
7	67.36	72.67	36	39.30	44.17
8	66.37	71.68	37	38.35	43.20
9	65.38	70.68	38	37.40	42.24
10	64.39	69.69	39	36.46	41.27
11	63.40	68.70	40	35.52	40.31
12	62.41	67.71	41	34.58	39.35
13	61.43	66.72	42	33.64	38.40
14	60.44	65.73	43	32.70	37.45
15	59.46	64.74	44	31.77	36.50
16	58.48	63.76	45	30.85	35.56
17	57.50	62.77	46	29.92	34.62
18	56.54	61.79	47	29.00	33.68
19	55.59	60.81	48	28.10	32.76
20	54.63	59.83	49	27.20	31.83
21	53.68	58.85	50	26.31	30.91
22	52.72	57.87	51	25.43	30.00
23	51.76	56.89	52	24.55	29.09
24	50.81	55.90	53	23.69	28.20
25	49.85	54.92	54	22.84	27.30
26	48.89	53.94	55	22.00	26.42
27	47.93	52.96	56	21.16	25.54
28	46.97	51.98	57	20.34	24.67

Age	Males	Females	Age	Males	Females
58	19.54	23.81	82	5.72	7.42
59	18.75	22.95	83	5.38	6.97
60	17.97	22.12	84	5.05	6.53
61	17.21	21.30	85	4.75	6.11
62	16.46	20.49	86	4.46	5.71
63	15.74	16.69	87	4.19	5.34
64	15.03	18.90	88	3.94	5.00
65	14.35	18.12	89	3.72	4.67
66	13.69	17.37	90	3.51	4.36
67	13.05	16.63	91	3.33	4.08
68	12.43	15.90	92	3.15	3.82
69	11.83	15.18	93	3.02	3.61
70	11.24	14.48	94	2.93	3.41
71	10.68	13.80	95	2.83	3.22
72	10.13	13.12	96	2.72	3.05
73	9.60	12.47	97	2.56	2.90
74	9.09	11.84	98	2.43	2.76
75	8.61	11.23	99	2.27	2.61
76	8.13	10.62	100	2.18	2.46
77	7.68	10.03	101	2.08	2.31
78	7.25	9.47	102	2.09	2.15
79	6.84	8.92	103	1.86	2.08
80	6.44	8.40	104	1.64	1.97
81	6.07	7.90	105	1.30	1.81

Appendix 7: Staircase of Investment Risk

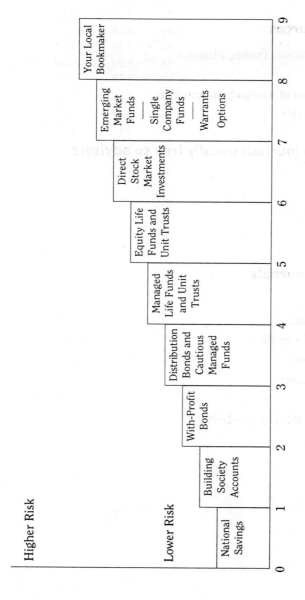

Higher Risk

Lower Risk

| | | | | | | | | | |
|0|1|2|3|4|5|6|7|8|9|

National Savings

Building Society Accounts

With-Profit Bonds

Distribution Bonds and Cautious Managed Funds

Managed Life Funds and Unit Trusts

Equity Life Funds and Unit Trusts

Direct Stock Market Investments

Emerging Market Funds

Single Company Funds

Warrants

Options

Your Local Bookmaker

Appendix 8: Information Sources for Financial Advisers

Electronic sources

The Exchange/Common Trading Platform
Prestel On-Line
Numerous providers of mortgage information
The World Wide Web

Weekly trade journals usually free to advisers

Money Market
Financial Adviser
Investment Weekly
Investment Adviser

Other trade journals

Money Facts
Business Money Facts
Life & Pensions Money Facts
Money Management
Pensions Management
Planned Savings
Savings Market (published quarterly)

Appendix 9: Lifestyle Questionnaire

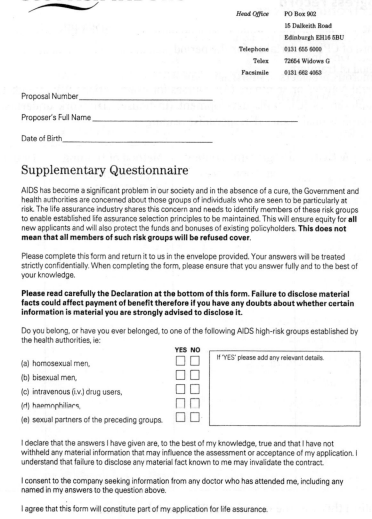

SCOTTISH WIDOWS

Scottish Widows' Fund and
Life Assurance Society

Head Office

PO Box 902
15 Dalkeith Road
Edinburgh EH16 5BU

Telephone   0131 655 6000
Telex   72654 Widows G
Facsimile   0131 662 4053

Proposal Number_____

Proposer's Full Name _____

Date of Birth_____

Supplementary Questionnaire

AIDS has become a significant problem in our society and in the absence of a cure, the Government and health authorities are concerned about those groups of individuals who are seen to be particularly at risk. The life assurance industry shares this concern and needs to identify members of these risk groups to enable established life assurance selection principles to be maintained. This will ensure equity for **all** new applicants and will also protect the funds and bonuses of existing policyholders. **This does not mean that all members of such risk groups will be refused cover.**

Please complete this form and return it to us in the envelope provided. Your answers will be treated strictly confidentially. When completing the form, please ensure that you answer fully and to the best of your knowledge.

Please read carefully the Declaration at the bottom of this form. Failure to disclose material facts could affect payment of benefit therefore if you have any doubts about whether certain information is material you are strongly advised to disclose it.

Do you belong, or have you ever belonged, to one of the following AIDS high-risk groups established by the health authorities, ie:

	YES	NO	
(a) homosexual men,	☐	☐	If 'YES' please add any relevant details.
(b) bisexual men,	☐	☐	
(c) intravenous (i.v.) drug users,	☐	☐	
(d) haemophiliacs,	☐	☐	
(e) sexual partners of the preceding groups.	☐	☐	

I declare that the answers I have given are, to the best of my knowledge, true and that I have not withheld any material information that may influence the assessment or acceptance of my application. I understand that failure to disclose any material fact known to me may invalidate the contract.

I consent to the company seeking information from any doctor who has attended me, including any named in my answers to the question above.

I agree that this form will constitute part of my application for life assurance.

Signature of Applicant_____ Date _____

Appendix 10: CPD Record Sheet

SOFA continuing professional development progress record

Name .... SOFA PIN ....

Record of CPD undertaken for the period .... to ....

Method of training:

General courses or seminars (A); courses for examinations (B); attendance at conferences (C); skills development (in-house) (D); work undertaken with professional bodies (E); specialist reading (F).

Date	Activity	Programme content and objectives	Method of training (please indicate A, B, C, D, E or F)	Hours

I confirm this is a true record of CPD undertaken by me.

Signed .... Date ....

Appendix 11: With-Profit Bonds: Market Value Adjusters (MVAs)

Almost all with-profit bonds include in the small print a market value adjuster. This unwelcome but necessary provision is included to protect remaining investors should some wish to cash in their bonds at a time when the stock market is or has been falling rapidly, when the with-profit fund will need to liquidate stock quickly, thus possibly incurring losses and expenses. These could either be borne by the fund, in which case existing investors would suffer, or be passed on to those generating the cost, namely investors withdrawing from the fund. MVAs are designed to protect the fund for the benefit of existing investors.

The latest 'Survey on With-Profit Bonds' by *Money Management* in December 1997 listed 23 product providers of which nine guarantee not to apply an MVA on tenth-year anniversaries. The number drops to two for fifth-year anniversaries. Only eight companies have applied an MVA within the last five years.

Some companies guarantee not to levy an MVA in the circumstance of a bond being encashed on the death of a holder; others guarantee not to apply an MVA in instances of regular withdrawals.

While the inclusion of the MVA is unwelcome, there is really no alternative in the interests of all investors in a life fund. The scenario demonstrates the general merit of spreading investment risk and not having too many eggs in one basket, so as in this case to avoid having to encash a with-profit bond at the wrong time, which might then trigger the application of an MVA.

Appendix 12: Individual Savings Accounts (ISAs)

Throughout the book the writer has deliberately not included technical data on individual savings or protection policies because we are primarily concerned with the general approach to giving investment advice. However, some technical notes are included on ISAs here because of their announcement in the March 1998 Budget and the major impact that they will have on the financial services industry.

- ISAs start on 6 April 1999 and are guaranteed to run for at least ten years. PEPs will be closed to new money from that date but all existing PEPs remain 'ring fenced' indefinitely and their existing exemption from income tax and CGT remains.

- Income from ISAs is free from income tax and any capital gain is free from CGT. In addition a 10 per cent credit will be paid for the first five years on dividends from UK equities.

- It will be possible to put cash (including National Savings), life insurance and stocks and shares into ISAs.

- The annual contribution limit is £5,000, with a maximum of £1,000 in cash and £1,000 in life assurance. For the 1999/2000 tax year the contribution limit is raised to £7,000 – with a cash limit of £3,000.

- There is no lifetime contribution limit.

- There is no minimum subscription.

- Investors have instant access to cash and investments without loss of tax benefits.

- Investors may have different ISA plan managers for each of the cash, shares and life insurance components if they wish.

- Windfall shares will not be eligible for transfer to an ISA.

- Investors must be aged 18 or over.

- Husbands and wives can have individual ISAs.

Other points worth noting are:

- The present single-company PEP scheme has been abolished.

- It will be possible to start a TESSA up to 6 April 1999, run it for the usual five years and then transfer the original capital of (up to) £9,000 to an ISA in addition to the usual subscription of £5,000 in that year.

- PEP mortgages seem set to continue as at present, but will instead be known as ISA mortgages.
- ISA providers have yet to announce the precise terms of their products, including the charging structure, so investors should check carefully that the tax advantages are not outweighed by any management fees.
- The full range of ISAs and individual product details remain to be finalised and published prior to 6 April 1999.

Appendix 13: Specimen Risk Warning for EZPTs, EIS and VCTs

RISK WARNING NOTICE (STANDARD LETTER 8 (4/95)

Investments in Enterprise Zone Property Unit Trusts (EZPUTs), Property Enterprise Trusts (PETs), Enterprise Trusts (ETs) and Capital Venture Trusts (CVTs)

This warning notice draws your attention to the risks associated with investments such as those listed above.

As with property in general, the value of the investment can go down as well as up. Many tax shield investments, of which these are prime examples, are subject to an initial price distortion as a result of the tax allowances and other benefits available; it may often be necessary to pay a higher price for such a property or other investment than for similar items not carrying such benefits.

EZPUTs are established to be held as an investment for long periods of time (25 years is typical). Although mechanisms may be available to enable the underlying property to be realised during this period, you may have difficulty in selling your investment before realisation of the underlying property, and you should not invest in an EZPUT, PET, ET or CVT if you may need to sell your investment prematurely.

There is no established market in EZPUTs, PETs, ETs or CVTs and you may have difficulty in selling or obtaining reliable information about your investments. The tax shields remain in place only if the investments are maintained for the statutory period; in the case of ETs and CVTs this is five years. Accordingly, you should carefully consider whether such an investment is appropriate to your circumstances.

I have received the risk warning notice set out.

Signed ....

Dated ....

I am also aware that the situation has changed considerably since FIMBRA designed this warning in September 1992. I am in full receipt of all the conditions concerning this particular investment and know that, firstly, this was primarily for each EZPUT and here the exit conditions were relaxed to seven years in March 1994. Secondly, subsequent Budgets and Treasury announcements have resulted in considerable expansion in the area of Enterprise and Venture Trusts such that there are an increasing number of arrangements to market such investments at the earliest exit dates allowable.

Appendix 14: National Savings 'Quick Guide'

	Rate of return	Tax position	Special features	Minimum	Maximum	Who may invest	Repayment terms	Direct purchase address
Premium Bonds	Prize fund 5.0%	TAX FREE	Odds fixed at 19,000 to 1 per £1 bond. Over 500,000 prizes per month. Top monthly prize of £1 million. Bonds eligible for prize draws one clear month after purchase.	£100	£20,000	Individuals over 16. Under 16, by parents, guardians, grandparents and great-grandparents.	Allow at least 8 working days.	Premium Bonds National Savings Blackpool FY3 9YP
13th Issue Index-linked Savings Certificates	Index-linking plus guaranteed Extra Interest of 2.25% compound when held for 5 years.	TAX FREE — Free of UK Income Tax at all rates and Capital Gains Tax.	A guaranteed real return in addition to Inflation-proofing, fixed for 5 years.	£100 Larger purchases can be for any amount within holding limit.	£10,000 No limit on reinvesting matured Certificates and Ulster Savings Certificates.	Individuals (also jointly), trustees, charities, some clubs and voluntary bodies.	Allow at least 8 working days. No interest if repaid in first year (except Reinvestment Certificates). If held less than 5 years, see Prospectus.	Savings Certificates National Savings Durham DH99 1NS
46th Issue Fixed Interest Savings Certificates	4.8% compound guaranteed when held for 5 years. General Extension Rate for matured Certificates = 3.51%.	TAX FREE — Free of UK Income Tax at all rates and Capital Gains Tax.	Fixed return for 5 years.	£100 Larger purchases can be for any amount within holding limit.	£10,000 No limit on reinvesting matured Certificates and Ulster Savings Certificates.	Individuals (also jointly), trustees, charities, some clubs and voluntary bodies.	Allow at least 8 working days. No interest if repaid in first year (except Reinvestment Certificates). If held less than 5 years, see Prospectus.	Savings Certificates National Savings Durham DH99 1NS
Children's Bonus Bonds Issue J	6.0% compound guaranteed when held for first 5 years. Further guaranteed returns notified before each following fifth anniversary. (No more returns after holder's 21st birthday.)	TAX FREE — Free of UK Income Tax at all rates and Capital Gains Tax.	No tax liability on parents' gifts.	£25 Then in units of £25.	£1,000 per issue.	Anyone over 16 for individuals under 16. (No trust holdings.)	Allow at least 8 working days for repayment at 5-year anniversary points or 21st birthday. No interest if repaid in first year. Otherwise 5% if repaid before 5th anniversary.	Children's Bonus Bonds National Savings Glasgow G58 1SB
FIRST Option Bonds	6.5% gross guaranteed to first anniversary (= 5.2% net). £20,000+ earns bonus of 0.25% gross (0.2% net). Further guaranteed rates notified annually. (Tax paid rates assume tax at 20%.)	Tax (at 20%) deducted at source. No further liability for basic or lower rate taxpayers.	Rates guaranteed 12 months at a time. Bonds can be held indefinitely.	£1,000 Larger purchases can be for any amount within holding limit.	£250,000 sole or joint.	Individuals sole or joint. Over 16; two jointly; trustees for not more than two individuals.	Allow a few days. No penalty for repayments at anniversary dates. Otherwise half interest since last anniversary. No interest if repaid in first year.	FIRST Option Bonds National Savings Glasgow G58 1SB
Capital Bonds Series L	6.0% compound guaranteed when held for 5 years. Gross.	Taxable but credited in full without deduction of tax at source. Fixed return for 5 years. All holders get gross interest automatically - no Inland Revenue registration form for non-taxpayers to fill in.		£100 Larger purchases can be for any amount within holding limit.	£250,000 Applies to total holdings from Series B onwards.	Individuals; two individuals jointly; trustees for not more than two individuals.	Allow two weeks. No interest if repaid in first year. If held less than 5 years, see Prospectus.	Capital Bonds National Savings Glasgow G58 1SB
Pensioners Bonds	6.1% ... paid monthly.	Taxable but credited in full without deduction of tax at source. Regular monthly income. All holders get gross interest automatically - no Inland Revenue registration form for non-taxpayers to fill in.		£500 Larger purchases can be for any amount within holding limit.	£50,000 (£100,000 jointly) in addition to holdings of any earlier Series.	Individuals (or two jointly) two individuals over 60; trustees for not more than two individuals over 60.	60 days notice with no interest during notice period - except at 5-year anniversaries. Or without notice but with penalty equal to 90 days interest. Repayment by crossed warrant direct to account.	Pensioners Bonds National Savings Blackpool FY3 9YP
Income Bonds	Under £25,000 7.0% gross £25,000+ 7.25% gross Rates variable.	Taxable but credited in full without deduction of tax at source. Regular monthly income. All holders get gross interest automatically - no Inland Revenue registration form for non-taxpayers to fill in.		£2,000 (£1,000 for further purchases). Larger purchases can be for any amount within holding limit.	£250,000 sole or joint.	Individuals; two jointly; trustees for not more than two individuals.	3 months notice without penalty. Or without notice but with penalty equal to 90 days interest. Repayment by crossed warrant.	Income Bonds National Savings Blackpool FY3 9YP
Investment Account	Under £500 4.75% gross £500+ 5.25% gross £2,500+ 5.5% gross £5,000+ 5.75% gross £10,000+ 6.0% gross £25,000+ 6.25% gross £50,000+ 6.5% gross Rates variable.	Taxable but credited in full without deduction of tax at source. All holders get gross interest automatically - no Inland Revenue registration form for non-taxpayers to fill in. Bank book records all transactions.		£20	£100,000	Individuals; sole or joint. Individuals jointly; not more than two trustees for not more than two individuals.	One month's notice. Or without notice but with penalty equal to 30 days interest.	Investment Account National Savings Glasgow G58 1SB
Ordinary Account	2.0% Standard rate 3.0% Higher rate Higher rate paid for each calendar month £500 or more held in account.	TAX FREE — No UK Income Tax on first £70 (£140 joint) annual interest.	Interest earned for whole calendar months. Interest credited every 31 Dec.	£10	£10,000	Individuals; two individuals jointly; not more than two trustees for not more than two individuals.	Up to £100 on demand. (Regular customer accounts: up to £250 at chosen post office.) For larger amounts allow a few days.	Ordinary Account National Savings Glasgow G58 1SB
Treasurer's Account	£10,000-£24,999 6.0% gross £25,000-£99,999 6.25% gross £100,000 6.5% gross Note: Balances under £10,000 3.0%. Rates variable.	Taxable but credited in full without deduction of tax at source.	Postal notification of interest rate changes. Transactions by telephone. Annual tax statements. Monthly statements following transactions.	£10,000 opening deposit.	£2 million per organisation.	Non-profit-making organisations.	30 days notice. Or without notice but with penalty equal to 30 days interest. Repayment by BACS.	Treasurer's Account National Savings Durham DH99 1NS

Appendix 15: The Mortgage Code

What is the Code?

The Mortgage Code sets the minimum standards of service that borrowers can expect from mortgage lenders and intermediaries which subscribe to the Code.

The Code's key commitments

The Code has ten key commitments. These will specify that lenders and intermediaries will –

- act fairly and reasonably in all dealings with you;
- ensure that all services and products comply with this Code, even if they have their own terms and conditions;
- give you information on services and products in plain language, and offer help if there is any aspect which you do not understand;
- unless you have already decided on your mortgage, help you to choose a mortgage to fit your needs;
- help you to understand the financial implications of a mortgage;
- help you to understand how your mortgage account works;
- ensure that the procedures staff follow reflect the commitments set out in this Code;
- correct errors and handle complaints speedily;
- consider cases of financial difficulty and mortgage arrears sympathetically and positively;
- ensure that all services and products comply with relevant laws and regulations.

Choosing a mortgage

The section on helping you to choose a mortgage explains that there are three different levels of service which might be given. These are **advice and a recommendation** as to which of the mortgages available from the lender or via the intermediary is most suitable for you, **information on the different types of mortgage product** on offer so that you can make an informed choice of which to take, or **information on a single mortgage**

product only, if only one mortgage is offered or if you have already made up your mind.

Whichever level of service is provided, you should find that before you finalise your mortgage you have been given information on all the following aspects. (If you are unclear about any of these, check with the lender or intermediary who is arranging your mortgage):

- the repayment method and the repayment period
- the financial consequences of repaying the mortgage early
- the type of interest rate – variable, fixed, discounted etc
- what your future repayments after any fixed or discounted period may be
- whether you have to take any insurance services with the mortgage, and if so whether the insurance must be arranged by the lender/ intermediary
- the general costs and fees which might be involved with the mortgage – valuation fees, arrangements fees, legal fees etc
- whether your selected mortgage terms can be continued if you move house
- when your account details may be passed to credit reference agencies
- mortgage interest tax relief
- whether you are required to pay a high percentage lending fee, and if so what this means to you

If you are using the services of a mortgage intermediary to arrange the loan, you should also be told if they are receiving a fee from the lender for the introduction of the mortgage, and whether they usually arrange mortgages from a selection of preferred lenders or from the market as a whole.

Compliance with the Code

Compliance with the Mortgage Code is monitored independently. In addition, any organisation subscribing to the Code must be a member of a recognised complaints scheme – the Banking Ombudsman, the Building Societies Ombudsman, or the Mortgage Code Arbitration Scheme. Your lender or intermediary will be able to tell you which scheme applies.

Copies of the Mortgage Code are available from your mortgage lender or mortgage intermediary.

Appendix 16: Networks

Networks are available to IFAs only. The concept is not applicable to 'tied' advisers. Networks were first formed in the early 1980s in order to help smaller IFAs with the increasing problems connected with operating as individuals/sole traders or as small partnerships that lacked the time and resources to be able to deal effectively with:

- training and compliance;
- research as to best products;
- administration generally.

In addition, because of their size and through economies of scale, networks may be able to:

- negotiate enhanced commission levels;
- arrange professional indemnity on more favourable terms;
- sometimes provide special software packages;
- sometimes offer centralised administration services.

Networks charge a fee based upon each member's annual turnover. The level of fee varies between networks in accordance with the range of services provided. For readers considering joining a network, it is appropriate to mention that most require two years' relevant experience, plus full FPC, and may in addition request applicants to demonstrate competence.

The writer, employed in a solicitors' practice, is precluded from joining a network and therefore has no first-hand experience of this way of working. Nevertheless, from conversations with IFAs, it seems that network members vary in their opinions of the benefits. Generally, the newer the adviser in financial services, the more likely he or she is to find the support and help of a network to be beneficial.

Appendix 17: Some Generic Files Kept by the Author

Annuities

AVC & FSAVCs

Children, Investments for

CIC

Distribution Bonds

Emerging Markets

Endowment Policies

EZPTs & EIS

Equities:

    Low-Cost Share Dealing

    Shareholder Perks

    Guaranteed Equity Plans

Equity Release

Ethical Investments

'Guaranteed' Investment Products

Home Income Plans

IHT

Impaired Lives

Income Drawdown

Income Tax Matters

Investor Protection

Investment in Second-Hand Life Policies

Investment Bonds

Keyman Cover

LTC

Mortgages Generally

National Savings

National Insurance Benefits

Offshore Investments

OEICS

Pensions

PEPs

PHI

PMI

Portfolio Planning

Regular Savings Plans

'Risk'

School Fees Planning

Selling Endowment Policies

SERPS

Share Exchange

Strength of Life Offices

Term Cover

TESSAs

Top Slicing

Tracker Funds

Trusts

Unit Trusts

VCTs

Viatical Settlements

WOP

Warrants

With-Profits Bonds

Index

Note: abbreviations listed on pages x and xi and financial qualifications listed on page xiv are excluded, as are references to the Financial Services Act and Financial Services Authority as both are so numerous.

LAW IN PRACTICE SERIES

from

Old Bailey Press
The New Publishers for Practitioners

This text is part of the new and dynamic *Law in Practice Series*.

The series comprises a range of *Concise Texts* dealing with recent developments in key mainstream areas of legal practice and providing a pathway through some of the more complex areas of contemporary legal practice (eg residential tenancies, financial services).

The *Concise Texts* have a number of features which give them a dynamism relevant to contemporary practice including the following:

- Topical, relevant and up-to-date
- Written for practitioners
- Clear and direct writing style
- Evaluative commentary
- Authors with relevant practice experience
- Support materials for Holborn College CPD courses
- Time-efficient reading
- Outstanding value for money

Further, the *Law in Practice Series* includes a number of specialist texts on some of the fast-emerging areas of contemporary legal practice.

Full details of the series is set out below.

Concise Texts	ISBN	Price
Commercial Property	1-85836-283-0	£6.95
Employment Law	1-85836-291-1	£6.95
European Union Law	1-85836-297-0	£6.95
Identifying Current Private Residential Tenancies	1-85836-288-1	£6.95
Introduction to Financial Services	1-85836-287-3	£6.95

Residential Tenancies	1-85836-086-2	£6.95
Small Private Companies	1-85836-292-X	£6.95
Wills and Probate	1-85836-295-4	£6.95

Forthcoming Concise Texts	ISBN	Price
Civil Litigation	1-85836-285-7	£6.95
Conveyancing	1-85836-286-5	£6.95
Crime and Criminal Procedure	1-85836-290-3	£6.95
Entertainment Licensing Law and Practice	1-85836-334-9	£9.95
Guide to the Human Rights Act 1998	1-85836-336-5	£6.95
Matrimonial and Child Care Law	1-85836-296-2	£6.95
Taxation	1-85836-293-8	£6.95

Other Titles	ISBN	Price
Environmental Law Guide	1-85836-079-X	£26.95
EU Law Today	1-85836-271-7	£14.95
A Guide to the Trusts of Land and Appointment of Trustees Act 1996	1-85836-267-9	£12.95
Materials Sourcebook on Environmental Law	1-85836-077-3	£23.95
Research on the Net	1-85836-269-5	£19.95

To complete your order, please fill in the form below:

Books required	ISBN	Quantity	Price	Cost
		Postage		
		TOTAL		

For UK, add 10% postage and packing.
For Europe, add 15% postage and packing.

ORDERING

By telephone to: Mail Order at 0171 385 3377, with your credit card to hand

By fax to: 0171 381 3377 (giving your credit card details)

By post to: Old Bailey Press, 200 Greyhound Road, London W14 9RY

When ordering by post, please enclose full payment by cheque or banker's draft, or complete the credit card details below.

We aim to despatch your books within three working days of receiving your order.

Name

Address

Postcode   Telephone

Total value of order, including postage: £

I enclose a cheque/banker's draft for the above sum, or

Charge my ☐ Access/Mastercard ☐ Visa ☐ American Express

Card number ☐☐☐☐ ☐☐☐☐ ☐☐☐☐ ☐☐☐☐

Expiry date ☐☐☐☐

Signature: ....Date: ....